Navigating the Glass Maze

Navigating the Glass Maze

◆

Phenomenological Interviews with Graduate Students of Adult Education Diagnosed with Attention-Deficit/ Hyperactivity Disorder

Tad A. Vogl, Ed.D.

iUniverse, Inc.
New York Lincoln Shanghai

Navigating the Glass Maze
Phenomenological Interviews with Graduate Students of Adult Education Diagnosed with Attention-Deficit/Hyperactivity Disorder

iUniverse books may be ordered through booksellers or by contacting:

iUniverse
2021 Pine Lake Road, Suite 100
Lincoln, NE 68512
www.iuniverse.com
1-800-Authors (1-800-288-4677)

Because of the dynamic nature of the Internet, any Web addresses or links contained in this book may have changed since publication and may no longer be valid.

The views expressed in this work are solely those of the author and do not necessarily reflect the views of the publisher, and the publisher hereby disclaims any responsibility for them.

ISBN: 978-0-595-44617-9 (pbk)
ISBN: 978-0-595-71126-0 (cloth)
ISBN: 978-0-595-88941-9 (ebk)

Printed in the United States of America

In memory of Distinguished Teaching Professor, John Niemi, Ed.D.

Contents

PREFACE

Navigating the Glass Maze offers the reader an inside look at how one academic, diagnosed with Attention-Deficit/Hyperactivity Disorder (AD/HD), set out to learn from others with whom he held in common, a neurological disorder as well as a lifelong investment in education.

I am that academic. Using a method of in-depth phenomenological interviewing, I was able to reveal seven essential meanings integral to the lives of four graduate students of adult education, all diagnosed with AD/HD in adulthood. In the first chapter, I introduce the impetus behind my study, the evolution of my central question, and my basic argument as to why such a forward-thinking discussion of higher education is important. Mindful of the need to establish context, I use the second chapter to place this study alongside three relevant literary strands. These include: characteristics of the adult learner, self-regulated learning, and learning from within AD/HD. In Chapter 3, I introduce phenomenology; I present the structure of my study; and I detail some of the problematic intricacies involved in having chosen a phenomenological method. [To avoid the sense of disjointedness that often accompanies efforts aimed at ensuring gender neutrality, I have elected to use feminine pronouns in Chapter 2 and masculine ones in Chapters 3 and 10.] Aware of the potential for bias to infiltrate my findings, I use Chapter 4 to examine the meanings I made of my own experiences with formal education. I hope that my efforts to ensure separation of my own perceptions from those of my informants—as well as those derived through analysis—will be evident. Chapters 5 through 8 feature the learning profiles of my informants: Marianne, Diane, Howard, and Karl (three doctoral candidates and one master's student). A limited amount of editing was necessary to promote the unimpeded flow of ideas and to clarify each person's original intent. The profiles were segmented according to major points of transition within the common life experience. At the end of each, I offer my observations regarding the person's self-understanding. Chapter 9 details the most apparent themes to emerge from the interviews. These include: motivation, the impact of personal and societal interests, the impact of the environmental structure, and the use of compensatory strategies. At chapter's end, I synthesize these themes into the seven essential meanings. Chapter 10 revisits my central question and addresses the myriad of other issues raised by conducting such a study. It also organizes the seven essential meanings into an educational model of graduate students diagnosed with AD/HD. The final chapter offers a candid snapshot of my personal and professional thoughts on what this study has meant, and it bids farewell to Marianne, Diane, Howard, and Karl.

This book represents nearly five years of research, which culminated in the completion of my doctoral dissertation in adult continuing education. Had I published my dissertation in full, my prospective audience would have been far smaller than I now hope. What appears here is an abridgement—some of which I reworked to appeal to broader interests. The title, *Navigating the Glass Maze*, holds special significance for me. Having gone many years without any explanation for my seemingly unique way of knowing and interacting, I have continuously had to navigate an ever-present onslaught of confusing barriers, unseen and often misunderstood, yet frustratingly familiar to anyone living with AD/HD.

ACKNOWLEDGEMENTS

There are numerous individuals whose belief, encouragement, and (at times) mere presence helped to guide me through what has been a sporadically intense and oftentimes confounding journey. Foremost, I wish to thank my advisor and mentor, Dr. Gene Roth, who showed great patience whenever mine went missing. Thank you to Dr. Paul Ilsley, whose stark challenges and comparatively subtle assurances served to strengthen my resolve. Thank you to Dr. Jorge Jeria, who joined my advisory committee at the eleventh hour. Thank you to my parents, Drs. Robert and Sonia Vogl, for countless hours spent listening, offering insightful feedback and criticism, editing, and entertaining their grandson whenever I needed the wide-open space of their farm in which to *think in motion*. Thank you to my wife, Julie, my stepson, Daniel, and my exuberant little boy, Hunter. You have each helped (and sacrificed) to make the fruition of this dream possible. Thanks to my lifelong friend, Varouge Mesrobian, who selflessly endured many hours of rambling monologues (in spite of an inexplicably high incidence of *accidentally dropped* calls). Thanks to my "big" sister, Linnea Vogl, who has always been able to pinpoint the inherent humor in otherwise stressful situations. Thanks to Gary Hubbard, who believed in my potential (even as I wavered). Thanks to Drs. (Uncle) Roland and (Aunt) Birgit Wolff, for their strident and cheerful forthrightness. Thanks to James Bosch, whose encouragement—though given over a decade ago—has remained fresh in my mind. Thanks to Kate Burch, John Fafinski, Dennis Graf, David Key, Tom Rairdon, and everyone else at The Larkin Center who provided workplace support. Thanks to Amy Cotter for that one final push (several times over). Thanks to Dr. Irving Seidman for devising a phenomenological research method that made perfect sense (to someone with AD/HD). Finally, I would like to express a hearty thank-you to my volunteers: Marianne, Diane, Howard, and Karl, respectively. I wish you each the very best.

1

APPROACHING THE GLASS MAZE

At age thirty I was tentatively diagnosed with Attention-Deficit/Hyperactivity Disorder (AD/HD). That I had recently begun taking doctoral courses in adult education was fortuitous, given my program's emphasis on self-regulated learning: a multi-faceted, self-knowledge-dependant process. Paired with the sense of ownership I increasingly exerted over my own education was a growing belief that other graduate students of adult education (similarly diagnosed) must surely possess an intriguing body of insight on what it meant to be an effective learner—in spite of living with a disorder at the center of so many opinions and disagreements. It was upon this conviction that I decided to investigate the meaning of formal learning from the perspective of individuals with whom I shared three key characteristics: a neurological disorder, a scholarly investment in adult education, and a determination to be the master of one's own learning.

Through experience, I knew that graduate students of adult education programs similar to that of my alma mater held a unique place from which to inform, shaped largely by their scholarly inclination for critical examination of the self-as-learner. Members of my dissertation committee, Drs. John Niemi and Gene Roth concurred that the content as well as the community of the adult education program at Northern Illinois University had a strong influence on their graduate students to understand and manage their own learning. Should any such student also happen to have AD/HD, our combined observations were that such a person should be in a position to offer meaningful and potentially instructive insight regarding AD/HD in higher education. At minimum, the intersection of personal experience with AD/HD and graduate programs in adult education had yet to be fully explored. With great personal interest, this intrepid exploration would map my journey into the world of doctoral research.

Six years into my program and equipped with energy bordering on urgency, I had yet to form a central question. Adding to the agony of my question's precise formulation was the warning given by committee member, Dr. Paul Ilsley. He informed me that despite any vitality of a strong central question, the qualitative researcher must understand that if the question is to remain relevant, it must be able to evolve as the research takes shape. Throughout the undulation of investigation and meaning-making, my guiding question ultimately solidified as: What meaning do graduate students of adult education programs, diagnosed with Attention-Deficit/Hyperactivity Disorder in adulthood, make of their formal learning experiences; and how do these meanings impact their understanding of themselves as learners?

Having established a worthwhile foundation for inquiry, the next logical question was: Whose interests would this study serve? At first, I envisioned a hodge-podge of candidates. They ranged from adults diagnosed with AD/HD to the professorate or administrators of formal adult education programs to a loose grouping of counselors, therapists, educators, and other professionals. I understand that for many, the identification of an audience would seem to be a straightforward task. For someone who has spent his entire life of forty-plus years living with AD/HD, however, any concept of straightforwardness borders on elusive. Stymied, I simply proceeded—confident that the authenticity of my topic would somehow lead to an interested party. As I neared completion of my dissertation, this question still lingered. In fact, the list of possibilities grew. Befuddled, and with time racing past in all directions, I reframed the question I could not answer. "For whom is this dissertation being written?" became "By whom might this dissertation be sought?" Almost immediately, the mental barrier I unwittingly constructed around this great unknown began to crumble. Spelled out amongst the rubble of rigidity was the obvious. The most appropriate audience had to be educational researchers. Whew! Next, it was time to identify the most suitable methodological approach.

During my enrollment, the adult education program at Northern Illinois University placed great value on using the self as a theoretical, living laboratory for critical thought and purposeful reflection—described by Knapp (1996) as the removal of oneself from the immediacy of a given experience such that new perspectives are possible. In the groundbreaking *The Meaning of Adult Education*, first published in 1926, author/educator Eduard C. Lindeman wrote that too much of learning consisted of vicarious substitution of someone else's experience. As an AD/HD adult in a non-AD/HD world, I observed that too much of everything consisted of someone else's experience. This perception led to my underlying contention that to get to the root of the AD/HD experience, one must begin with a person who has AD/HD. In this case, I was that person.

Given the dearth of available literature addressing my narrowly defined topic, any attempt to generalize what, at the time, amounted to little more than a biased smattering of informed guesswork would not only be premature, but also unlikely to garner serious peer consideration. Empiricism, therefore, was out—at least for the present. For the discussion to gain momentum, I would need to establish a convincing set of research-generated themes. How to proceed, however, would require quite a bit of investigative brainstorming.

On the subject of what makes for good qualitative research, I was intrigued with what I found. Alvesson and Skoldberg (2000) wrote that it ought to avoid definite statements about the way things are. Instead, it should place emphasis on having looked at a problem in a particular way. In place of reliability, validity, and the ability to generalize, there must be credibility, dependability, and authenticity—with the goal of understanding the ways in which subjects of the research interpret their own reality (Turnbull, 2002). Moreover, qualitative approaches have high potential for latent meanings to arise, given a well-researched phenomenon and thoughtful presentation. Furthermore, whatever method I chose, it would need to contain structural safeguards to keep me from impregnating the words of my informants with elements of my own worldview. Such a method would also need to be held in high enough esteem as to give my findings and subsequent conclusions merit.

Struggling to match my proposal with the most suitable method, Dr. Ilsley suggested that I consider phenomenology: a philosophic construct that posits the inseparability between a given phenomenon and human consciousness of it. Without any other leads and after having blithely agreed to give his suggestion some thought, I stumbled upon Brookfield's (1990) declaration that phenomenological methods were particularly well suited for inquiries involving the ways in which individuals become aware of how they learn. Presto! Despite a short-lived surge of relief, months of exasperation would separate me from my discovery of Irving Seidman's (1998) method of in-depth phenomenological interviewing. Of indescribable value to me was that his text was both plainspoken and engaging. I found his relaxed style enjoyable, very readable, and ultimately quite instructive. Most importantly, I learned how to use phenomenology as a means to uncover and develop one or more themes worthy of further investigation.

In preparation to conduct in-depth interviews, it was suggested that the researcher could benefit from personal experimentation not only as an interviewer but also as an interviewee. I took the suggestion a step further by finding a volunteer to interview me as though I were a participant in my own study. I hoped that in doing so, not only would I achieve a better idea of how to approach the impending interview process, but that it would help me to highlight my own beliefs concerning the phenomenon in question. I found the experience to be enlightening (and in no way flattering). By the time my research proposal was approved, and well before I established contact with any of the potential informants, I had already transcribed the practice interview, and was able to put it to use in the identification and description of several facets of my personal belief system, as they related to my study. It also helped me to explore my ideas and personal understandings of what it meant to be an adult living with AD/HD. This facet of my study would continue through completion of my dissertation.

Also possessing an accessible writing style, Creswell (1997) identified three possible goals of qualitative research. One was that it could seek to explore issues experienced by (or from the perspective of) a previously under-represented group. Another was that it could ferment an original way of looking at a problem. The third was that it could build upon the depth and breadth of the established subject-related literature. Ever since learning of Creswell's goals, it has been my aspiration to achieve all three.

2

MAPPING THE LITERARY STRANDS

As a researcher, it was imperative for me to seek linkages between my lines of reasoning and what others had reasoned before. However, in no way could I relegate this task to some set stage within the research process. Early on, my advisory committee forewarned of the jumble of junctures I would experience—and indeed, this was so. Oftentimes unforeseen jolts would send me reeling, only to have me trudge back and sort through it all time and again. Although three primary literary strands emerged as most relevant early on, throughout successive drafts of my dissertation my mind never dismissed the certainty that I would be drawn back to the literature regardless of how much I might have preferred otherwise. With the goal of fermenting a unitary foundation of understanding, I selected worthy passages with exquisite care—*Google Scholar* at my fingertips. The challenge I assigned myself was to weave the strands together in such a way as to highlight the connectedness that I understood as a student, as an adult educator, and as an individual living with AD/HD.

It is noteworthy to mention that given the considerable difficulties I have had with concentration and sustained effort throughout my lifetime, I have always been drawn to authors and speakers who possess the ability and willingness to present information in such a way as to capture and sustain one's attention. Whether accomplished through an especially accessible style of presentation, by way of having achieved a sense of timelessness, or by virtue of unconventionality, the result is similar: when reading something that speaks in a voice I recognize, my AD/HD "gremlins" are temporarily dispersed. Without question, this specific issue of literary accessibility to the AD/HD mind (mine in particular) has played a central role in the determination of who I chose to cite.

Characteristics of the Adult Learner

Learning can take place anywhere. For many people learning is, quite simply, a way of life. Others may seek new information on a need-to-know basis, for a sense of accomplishment, or for the recognition and/or benefits afforded by a diploma or certificate of completion. To many, if not most, college may seem to be an obvious example of adult education. Those most familiar with the practice of adult education and the characteristics of adult learners, however, know to look beyond the obvious. Within the practice of adult education, a person is an adult to the extent that she is currently performing roles typically assigned to adults and is essentially self-dependant (Knowles, 1980). This description alone would no doubt include a large number of traditional-aged college students, were it not for another presupposition of adult education. That is, those who enter college after having experienced the adult life-world for periods of variable length have characteristics that set them apart from those who enter straight from high school. The obvious difference is age. The more illustrative differences are less apparent.

Pedagogy (the practice of teaching children) predominates the transmittal of formal knowledge. Students are told what they need to know and what they must do to prove they know it. According to Freire (1972), the outcome of this teacher-centered mode of education is the establishment of a passive citizenry. Whether or not learner passivity is the intent, given pedagogy's strong emphasis on equipping students for the future, education is largely conceptualized as having more to do with what one hopes to become than with whom one presently is. Within this preparatory mindset, critical thinking and problem posing take a back seat to the acquisition of existing knowledge. Rather than helping students learn to formulate their own real-world questions from rigorous inspection of a given phenomenon, pedagogy directs students towards acceptance of someone else's conclusions, often based upon intentions of unknown origins. Despite reaching the age of maturity around the same time as the high-school-to-college transition, pedagogy—with its trappings of conformity and acquiescence—feels familiar and comfortable to many young adults.

Movement away from pedagogy gathers force as the young adult assumes a wider range of responsibility, accumulates a growing body of experience, and begins to more fully appreciate the rewards of taking ownership for her own affairs. From this point on, according to Knowles (1980), the pedagogical paradigm of "teacher knows best" is no longer adequate. The autonomous adult now has an experiential framework from which to determine what information is missing or needed. This adult also has a good idea of how the missing information could be put to use. At the very least, she understands that actionable knowledge has power. That is, once in possession of the right tools, meaningful action is within reach, even if the precise action has yet to be envisioned. Paradoxically, Knowles observed, many adult learners unwittingly succumb to the familiarity of the pedagogical teacher-student relationship the moment they reenter a classroom. They might challenge the teacher's knowledge, but not the teacher's role. In adult education, a facilitator of learning supplants the traditional role of teacher, per se, by assisting learners in the identification of personal goals as well as the most appropriate means for achieving them (Smith, Roland, Havens, and Hoyt, 1992).

Although adult education plainly has subject matter, Stanage (1987) clarified that it is not itself a specific discipline. The umbrella is far too encompassing. Despite the widely shared premise among scholars of adult education that a unifying theory of adult learning may avoid fruition indefinitely, numerous constructs, formulations, and models do exist (Brookfield, 1986; Merriam and Caffarella, 1991). Given its accessibility to me personally, I chose Knowles' (1980) *andrgogy* as the starting point from which to introduce several fundamental characteristics of adult learners.

Andragogy supposes five underlying assumptions, the first of which is that adults have a psychological need to be self-directing. Hoban and Hoban (2004) defined self-directed learning as a process whereby individuals initiate, manage, and evaluate learning projects without external assistance or oversight. This assumption posits that in most instances, adults prefer to have an active role in deciding the "how" and the "what" in their lives. Furthermore, successful experience with self-directed activity tends to promote additional experimentation. Evans and Miller (1990) found a clear and positive relationship between perceiving oneself as self-directed and the ability to manage one's personal affairs successfully. As people tend to develop a greater sense of their own identity as they age, older students are increasingly more likely to possess cognitive styles better adapted to the management of multiple tasks, pursuant to their interests and responsibilities.

With age comes experience, and the wider one's range of experience, the greater the possibility that one's past may inform one's present in some helpful way. This introduces the second andragogical assumption, that adults have a tendency to assign deeper meaning to what they have learned experientially as opposed to what they have acquired passively. A benefit of experience-based knowledge is that it provides a tangible context that learners can reflect upon at will. Taken further, individuals who use critical reflection to reexamine experience-driven assumptions, and who take specific action in response to any new-found perspectives, develop the confidence to articulate wants that are in line with their needs (Freire, 1972). Simply having the wherewithal to frame novel situations upon a foundation of prior understanding, however, does not necessarily mean that one's conclusions have been well reasoned. In cases where deeply held meanings are more accurately defined as biases or prejudices, for example, new understandings are certain to be flawed, or at the very least, obstructed (Polson, 1993).

Andragogy's third assumption is that adults will seek new information when experience tells them it is needed. Once affirmed as knowledge, its value is determined according to the extent to which one can put it to timely and effective use. Such immediacy of assessment speaks to the fourth assumption—a clear point of demarcation from the pedagogical model, where there exists a gulf between the acquisition and the application of knowledge. By organizing learning experiences around the development of competencies already in one's possession, the resulting knowledge is likely to be of use within the adult learner's present context, and therefore be held in higher esteem than learning experiences geared toward some speculative and distant future.

Some years after the introduction of his first four assumptions, Knowles added a fifth: that intrinsic motivations hold greater overall significance than external ones (McMillan, 2003). Although this assumption does not specifically address the widely held ideal of using adult education as a means to achieve social justice, it does acknowledge that the capacity to bring about desired change draws upon intrinsic values and motivations. Central to such an effort is the relational impact of critical thought upon purposeful action in which individuals question the validity of what society is willing to accept (Hart, 1992). Without such examination, as both Hart and Freire (1972) separately observed, the subordinate classes (though much greater in number) remain largely passive before an ideologically driven, hegemonic consensus maintained by the dominant class: those with the greatest concentration of wealth. This is by no means a new challenge for educators, nor is it likely to be resolved any time soon. Early in the twentieth century, for example, it was Dewey (1916) who observed that unless students were able to identify the truly important societal issues of the day, it was unlikely that they would muster the motivation necessary to seek out and illuminate specific causes of injustice and pair them with realistic and workable solutions. The implication for the socially conscious adult educator of today is that adult education requires something of the individual learner. At the basic level, when learners become active in their own education, they become potential resources for others. At the highest level, learners come to recognize that to be truly educated, one's possession of knowledge must be accompanied by ongoing, purposeful and informed application (Lindeman, 1926).

Self-Regulated Learning

In simple terms, self-regulated learning describes the conscious selection, assessment, and exchange or modification of one's learning strategies while engaged in a given activity. Although this concept is not new to formal teacher education, its influence is growing, with several interrelated factors helping to explain the rise in visibility. The first involves the time-tested expectation that present information will be updated or replaced with ever-increasing speed. To prevent adults from becoming antiquated depositories of yesterday's knowledge, they must learn how to establish a flexible and continuous method for remaining current (Kremer-Haylon and Tillema, 1999). Yet, unless they are given the proper tools, and until they assume their rightful place at the center of their own learning, a finely tailored and effective method is unlikely to materialize.

Built upon a base of self-understanding and combined with an ability to make well-reasoned judgments regarding one's own learning, the self-regulated are able to describe who they are as learners, their optimum conditions for learning, the skills and strategies they possess, as well as their limitations, whether actual or perceived (Pintrich, 2000). Continuous, accurate self-monitoring is essential. Questions are posed. "Is progress being made?" "Are intrusive thoughts or emotions being managed?" "Is motivation being maintained?" Such individuals consider what is or is not working and what they must be do to increase or improve knowledge acquisition and understanding in the present moment. Once formed, a planned response is immediately implemented, as self-regulated learning involves actual use of those skills and/or strategies deemed most relevant to the task at hand (Niemi, 2002). Cognizant of possible demand fluctuations, these individuals must be able to select and apply the most appropriate skills and strategies flexibly and without hesitation (Swanson, 1990). Self-regulated learning, therefore, involves much more than the internalization of some set of guiding principles. In essence, it involves the personalization of education. With all other elements in place, the linchpin for self-regulation is learner confidence.

The concept of believing in one's own ability to learn in a given situation, under certain conditions, is referred to as self-efficacy. Unlike self-esteem, self-efficacy is not so much an assessment of one's worthiness as it is a perception of one's ability to achieve within a given context. Even a person with low self-esteem—as Hoban and Hoban (2004) contend—may have an awareness of being able-bodied with regard to some particular task. Of the numerous influences that can affect self-efficacy, according to Bandura (1997), domain mastery provides the greatest potential for positive impact. Having consistently met with success in the past bolsters a person's confidence as she faces the same or similar task in the present. Conversely, the failure to achieve mastery when mastery is the goal has an opposite effect (Hoban and Hoban, 2004). An individual's perception of mastery, however, might not necessarily reflect reality. That is, a person could come to believe that she possesses an ability or talent in an area where she clearly does not. Neither is self-efficacy internally universal, as one's level of confidence may be high in one domain, yet low in another. It may even be affected by something as fleeting as mood shifts (Bandura, 1995).

Whereas the word *fleeting* is descriptive of something that passes swiftly and is gone, for large numbers of adults diagnosed with AD/HD, whose mood fluctuations have been described as burdensome (Brooks and Goldstein, 2006), that which disappears swiftly may be replaced just as swiftly. Even when at odds with actual ability, the greater one's perception of self-efficacy, the more likely one is to set high personal standards and maintain a commitment to them (Bandura, 1993). Furthermore, when learners believe in their ability to master academic pursuits, their aspirations, their levels of interest in intellectual activities, their academic accomplishments, and how well they prepare themselves for the future tend to be positively affected (Bandura, 1997). Whether or not the self-regulated learner achieves success consistently, she maintains ownership for the process as well as the outcome. Arguably, such determination to rise above adversity should lead to a reinvestment in the self-regulated learning process (Lidner and Harris, 1992).

One way of conceptualizing the self-regulated learner is as someone who has learned how to learn. An individualized and lifelong process, these learners acquire and modify their knowledge acquisition skills and problem-solving abilities. Thus equipped, they are able to seamlessly maintain their awareness, accurately monitor and adjust their performance, and critically reflect on present experience, while remaining mindful that each experience may be useful as a resource for further learning (Candy, 1990). Simply stated, learning how to learn refers to having or acquiring the knowledge and skills needed to learn effectively in virtually any situation (Smith, 1982).

Learning from Within AD/HD

Published in 2000, the *Diagnostic and Statistical Manual of Mental Disorders IV-Text Revision* (DSM-IV-TR) provides the medical standard for the diagnosis of Attention-Deficit/Hyperactivity Disorder (AD/HD), in which three primary types are recognized: the combined type, the predominantly inattentive type, and the predominantly hyperactive-impulsive type. Although some symptomatic overlap is relatively common, those diagnosed with the hyperactive-impulsive type have a greater tendency for uninhibited behaviors compared to the inattentive individuals who may seem overly controlled or even rigid. Where the hyperactive-impulsive individual will often attribute her situational difficulties to the actions and attitudes of others, the inattentive individual is often keenly aware of her deficits and may shoulder a sense of shame in response (Fisher, 1998). With respect to what is, perhaps, the most widely recognized characteristic (and namesake) of the hyperactive-impulsive type, Fisher offers a thought-provoking explanation: the boredom precipitating an individual's need for novel or anxiety-producing behaviors often stems from a sense of internal disorganization. Whether climbing onto the window ledge in the fourth grade or white water kayaking as an adult, the impetus for such behavior in the life of the AD/HD person is essentially the same. So too is the result: risky behavior demands at least a temporary state of internal organization.

Under various names through modern history AD/HD has been the most studied childhood psychiatric disorder in existence (Barkley, 1997). Despite the American Psychiatric Association's 1980 conclusion that AD/HD (at the time, referred to as Attention Deficit Disorder or ADD) could no longer be considered a disorder of childhood only, the implication that AD/HD might impact the lives of adults failed to gain widespread notice for nearly a decade.

Not too surprisingly, the suddenness with which adults began to be diagnosed in the early 1990's led to broad public skepticism. After all, many of the symptoms of AD/HD are quite common. People lose things. People become distracted. People experience impatience from time to time. Because of these and other observations, many have discounted AD/HD as a legitimate neurological disorder (Nadeau, 1995). Instead, such individuals have been described as underachieving, lazy, immature, or unmotivated (Brown, 2000). What a naysayer fails to appreciate is the extent to which prevalence and intensity can interfere with one's daily functioning. Much more than a smattering of temporary setbacks experienced at irregular intervals, the symptoms of AD/HD are illustrative of a chronic, lifetime disorder. Exacerbating their frustration is that many individuals with AD/HD are well aware that they possess prerequisites for success, and yet for reasons they do not understand—find their visions perpetually out of reach (Murphy, 1995).

In response to fears of over-diagnosis and consequent over-reliance on pre-scription medication, the American Medical Association has assured the public that the evidence in support of AD/HD is far more compelling than for most mental disorders (Goldman, Genel, Bezman, and Slanetz, 1998). With increased visibility and acceptance and the rapid expansion of available sources of informa-tion (including a staggering number of websites that cater to adult AD/HD), there exists an increasing danger of AD/HD becoming the self-diagnosis of choice for individuals who may have learned of the disorder through casual read-ing but who lack any depth of understanding (Biggs, 1995). A diagnosis of AD/ HD may also be more appealing to individuals who have a more serious (and thus, more stigmatizing) neurological problem.

As noted by Hartmann (1997), the high prevalence of AD/HD within fami-lies led some to equate symptoms with learned behaviors resulting from multi-generational familial dysfunction. Comparisons of familial to genetic factors, however, have shown that this is not the case (Goodman and Stevenson, 1989). Thus, the inevitable question is raised: If AD/HD has existed throughout the ages, why then has it become so polemical only recently? The apparent short answer has to do with context. Lahey (1998) suggested that behaviors symptom-atic of AD/HD might avoid the label of "dysfunctional" as long as expressed within compatible environments. To illustrate compatible versus incompatible environments Hartmann (1997) likened the modern classroom (where the indi-vidual with AD/HD typically struggles) to a farming society. He then compared this structured environment to the more loosely structured, hunting/gathering society, where the ability to continuously refocus one's attention in response to even the most subtle changes within the immediate environment would have been highly prized. Having provided the disclaimer that his "Hunter in a Farmer's World" paradigm is based upon personal reflection and does not consti-tute medical advice, his readership is nonetheless invited to reframe attentional disorders as attentional differences.

Upon Entering College

As noted by Jones, Kalivoda, and Higbee (1997), the majority of students diag-nosed with AD/HD who enter college are intelligent enough to graduate. In fact, it is not uncommon for some individuals with AD/HD to operate within the above average or gifted range (DSM-IV-TR, 2000). Nevertheless, certain obstacles can be anticipated, with undergraduate requirements in mathematics and foreign language being oft-cited examples (Richard and Chandler, 1994). For younger (diagnosed) students used to institutional advocacy, the shift to personal responsibility that accompanies adulthood may lead to other problems, thus making self-knowledge all the more desirable (Quinn, 2001). Although colleges that receive federal funds must avail some accommodation, the onus to come forward is on the individual (Latham and Latham, 1995). Although federal law does not require post-secondary schools to provide formal disability assessments, some schools do staff qualified professionals nonetheless. Other schools may recommend off-campus testing services. While most public colleges and universities do accept a medical diagnosis of a disability, a student seeking assistance must adhere to the more stringent, legal definition. To legally qualify as a disabled person, the individual's condition must be such that it renders the individual unable to perform a major life activity to the same level as an average person in the general population (Latham and Latham, 1997). Such a standard may well prove to be an impediment for a person of high intelligence and/or ability, however. Although she may be at a clear disadvantage when compared to others of similar intelligence (who do not have a disorder), the benchmark includes all persons, not just bright ones and importantly, not just college students (Latham and Latham, 1997).

Complicating the matter of measuring performance is the issue of idiosyncrasies. Whereas the inability to sustain attention in situations where sustained attention is expected is descriptive of the disorder, whether the individual exhibits the symptom hinges largely on the amount of interest she has in the subject. Even when subjects hold little interest, adults with AD/HD are often able to hide their symptoms (at least initially). As a task nears the middle or end, however, symptoms often become increasingly visible (Fisher, 1998). Examples of distracting stimuli, as drawn from personal testimony, abound in the literature. For example, imagine a person who is easily distracted by seemingly insignificant noises, changes in lighting or temperature, or a succession of random thoughts, yet able to become immersed and completely focused on a subject or activity of intrinsic interest. Although broad characteristic preferences, such as desiring outlets for physical activity, have been identified, specific attention-capturing interests can be as individual to the person as one person is to another.

Issues of advocacy aside, and whether or not they eventually earn their degrees, young adults with AD/HD are likely to feel overwhelmed by the sheer multitude of changes inherent within the transition from being cared and provided for to being increasingly—even abruptly—independent (Latham and

Latham, 1997). Naivety alone, however, may at least partially explain the vulnerability to underachievement, interpersonal difficulties, stress-overload, diminished self-esteem, and depression of many young adults (Schommer, 1998). Rather than providing an advantage over non-diagnosed students, the broad goal of accommodation services is to help level the playing field between all students relevant to their specific disability-related needs. That is not to suggest, however, that all students who qualify for assistance by virtue of having AD/HD necessarily use or even need the available assistance (Richard, 1995a). Especially as they mature, adults are ever more likely to have amassed (or fine-tuned) a range of characteristics that can make academic success possible. These include the comprehension and acceptance of their disability, the development of compensatory strategies, the setting of realistic goals, and the development of strong self-advocacy and interpersonal communication skills (Wolf, 2001). Although some students may not be aware of the existence of such programs on campus, others (some of whom feel stigmatized by their diagnosis) may simply choose not to use them (Katz, 2006).

Having Taken a Few Detours

It is only logical to assume that as the number of mature students returning to school increases, the possibility that greater numbers of adults with AD/HD entering college, diagnosed or not, must also be on the rise (Bramer, 1996). Before 1980, the psychiatric community gave no official acknowledgement that AD/HD could persist into adulthood. This fact, compounded by a nearly decade-long delay in the popular visibility of such a diagnosis, resulted in many older students remaining unaware of their specific condition well beyond the age of maturity. Thanks to intelligence, creativity, perseverance and other characteristics, some individuals have simply been able to manage their disorder without drawing attention to themselves. Others, including Hartmann (1997), have even associated certain benefits with having AD/HD. Those bright enough to have attended college who instead chose to enter the workforce are likely to have faced employment difficulties similar to what would have been faced in post-secondary school. As Wasserstein, Wasserstein, and Wolf (2001) point out, working adults must create internal structures to balance the demands of their occupations with their personal responsibilities. One result of having to manage the oftentimes multifaceted responsibilities inherent in day-to-day life for working adults is that they must learn to integrate and apply knowledge based upon real-world contexts and to make sound judgments based on actual evidence (Magolda, 2002). Given this reality, the quantity of practical experiences amplifies the older adult's ability to consider new information in a variety of contexts (Jehng, Johnson, and Anderson, 1993). Yet again, having AD/HD will likely have tempered any advantages inherent to the "work first and school second" paradigm. Poor time management alone frequently leads to showing up late, having problems completing paperwork, and missing deadlines (Wasserstein et al., 2001). Adults with AD/HD may also have trouble with occupations that provide limited opportunities for spontaneous movement (DSM-IV-TR, 2000). For those whose AD/HD has gone undetected, the accompanying sense of failure and intense frustration can lead to a state of learned helplessness: the belief that achievement is impossible, no matter the effort taken. Furthermore, as one's sense of success versus failure is inextricably linked to the conceptualization of innate ability, one may very well devalue personal accomplishments that would easily leave others brimming with pride (Murphy, 1995).

As workplaces have increasingly welcomed diversification, individuals with "specialized brains" have been able to find vocations that fit well with their particular interests, skill sets, and ways of knowing (Sandler, 1995). Nevertheless, each time someone with a neurological disorder reaches a new threshold of responsibility, previously unanticipated challenges are likely to emerge. Once breached, seeming workaholics may struggle just to keep pace (Weiss, 1996). For those with a history of success, an experience such as this may well be the trigger that sends them seeking help. Regardless, as a person ages the likelihood of a self-generated referral increases (Mapou, 2001).

Once an adult is diagnosed, increased opportunities may await. Following proper diagnosis, the individual has a realistic framework from which to reexamine past experience. In place of the sense of shame that frequently results from a long history of failing to meet expectations and/or falling short of one's goals (a common experience of the undiagnosed adult) the individual can begin working to dispel some of her self-critical and/or self-deprecating beliefs that often serve to compound and complicate actual symptoms (Fisher, 1998). Once aware of her limitations, the individual is better able to compensate for them using a new set of expectations (Mezirow, 1991). Described as a worthy developmental exercise, Richard (1995b) found that many college students have penned essays in which the subject of growing up with AD/HD was explored. Beyond serving to increase one's self-knowledge, these students found themselves in a better position from which to self-advocate. And the more willing a student is to confront those previously held values, beliefs, and behaviors that have caused (and/or continue to cause) difficulty or discomfort, the greater the likelihood that such an exercise will provide a boost to learning effectiveness. After all, the most meaningful learning is that which arises from a disquieting reassessment of our own lives (Brookfield, 1986).

Keeping Organized and Managing Time

Generally, it is not that students with AD/HD do not know what to do in a given situation. Rather, fundamental problems pertaining to self-regulation are at issue (Marone and Johnston, 2002). Persons with AD/HD do not actually lack the ability to pay attention; they just lack the ability to activate or sustain their attention upon demand. This is especially true when the task lacks intrinsic value. A person with AD/HD may be astutely aware that attending to some specific task is of great importance, yet lacking a visceral connection to the task, be unable to maintain focus. When a task (or activity) is of genuine interest, however, the same individual may be able to maintain intense focus for prolonged periods. In reference to the AD/HD population, such periods of intensity have commonly been referred to as *hyperfocus* (Brown, 2000).

Although the DSM-IV-TR does not mention negative emotion and mood regulation as part of the formal diagnostic criteria for AD/HD, diagnosed individuals have been found to exhibit greater mood variability, negative affect, and problems with managing stress when compared to control populations (Nigg, John, Blaskey and Huang-Pollock, Willcutt, Hinshaw, and Pennington, 2002). Rather than continuously wage battle with extraneous stimuli, one way that persons with AD/HD avoid becoming overwhelmed is to respond by doing nothing at all (Quinn, 2001). As bothersome stimuli is likely to accompany nearly any activity to some degree, deliberate inaction is quite capable of consuming large swaths of time. Even when the individual does manage to stay on task, she is unlikely to be able to complete a task at the same speed a person without AD/HD could (Fisher, 1998). Although it may be possible to substantially reduce the quality and quantity of extraneous distractions within a controlled environment, the individual's mind may still drift to other thoughts, causing the person to lose track of what she was doing or thinking. At other times, one's ability to attend has less to do with idiosyncratic distracters and more to do with a style of instruction out of step with the learner's needs. Through interviews of college, students with AD/HD, Willis, Hoben, and Myette (1995) were able to draw attention to one such mismatch. A student identified as Mike found it difficult to follow along in class unless the information was presented linearly. Had his instructors catered to his preferred way of absorbing information, he still would have been subject to the occasional barrier whenever a link in the chain of information did not make sense. For Mike, moving past the barrier and returning to it later would not have been a viable option. Quite simply, it did not work in his case. According to Quinn (2001), not only is self-knowledge important for effective self-advocacy within the college environment, but the more one knows about one's learning preferences generally, the more control one has over one's ability to learn in virtually any situation (Winne, 1995).

For many with AD/HD, the pressure of a deadline activates the ability to focus. Under different names, the pressure-or stress-fueled ability to focus has drawn mixed reviews. Whereas Weiss (1997) identified the tendency to over-focus as a difficulty associated with having AD/HD, Kelly and Ramundo (1993) have equated the concept of *hyperfocus* with the ability to problem-solve well under pressure. Ratey (2001) provided an illustrative example citing a woman who described her life as though she was trapped inside of a B-movie with all the technical glitches one would expect. It was only in response to heightened levels of stress that she was able to cast aside the discord. And the greater the stress, the more productive and focused she became.

Summary

This review identified three strands within the literature, each of which has helped to frame the phenomenon at the heart of this publication. Early on, I stated as an objective (for this chapter), the formulation of a foundation of understanding. In pursuit of this ideal, I sought to illuminate the connectedness of learning in adulthood, self-regulated learning, and learning from within AD/HD. Accordingly, five tenets of adult learning (collectively regarded as andragogy) were identified. Through this andragogical lens, it is apparent how self-regulated learning—where the individual has assumed personal control over her knowledge acquisition process—is necessary to fully escape the oftentimes comfortable bounds of pedagogy where teacher still knows best. An integral facet of self-regulation is self-knowledge. Whether or not one's means of acquiring knowledge appears to be conventional is not an issue. Knowing how one learns, under what conditions one learns, and having the tools to maximize one's learning effectiveness in any situation is.

That much of learning involves unlearning is a popular refrain. Within the context of this publication, a more meaningful conceptualization would be that much of one's self-efficacy is dependent upon unlearning. Specifically, ingrained invalidation must be unlearned. Given the length of time that AD/HD has been a subject of continuous inquiry, I found the extent to which students with AD/HD characteristics have been singled out as lazy, unmotivated, and/or willfully difficult to be astounding. What graduate programs in adult education (as described herein) have to offer learners of all types is the wherewithal and the opportunity to reframe past experience from a position of heightened self-awareness and a deeper self-understanding.

3

ADHERENCE TO PHENOMENOLOGICAL PRECEPTS

The central role of philosophy is to capture the essence of a phenomenon, through exploration, description, and through first-hand intuition (Stanage, 1987). The same might be said of phenomenology, a movement built upon the writings of German mathematician Edmund Husserl during the first half of the twentieth century. At its philosophic heart, phenomenology conceptualizes the reality of a phenomenon as being inextricably linked to the consciousness of it. Consequently, the underlying meaning or truth of a given phenomenon can only be accessed through the deliberate examination of lived experiences (Thomasson, 2005). The goal of all research should be to achieve greater understanding for humankind. In contrast to objectivistic models, interpretive methodologies explore the quality of an event, experience, or phenomenon. Rather than seeking to distill conclusions that may be generalized, phenomenological inquiry fosters a dialog between the examined and the examiner where the goal is to open doors to different ways of thinking—actionable within real-world contexts (Cooper, Gibson, Hanes, and Sundre, 2000). In short, what phenomenology provides is the possibility of being able to look at an existing problem from a previously undiscovered perspective. It is often used in research situations where the subject of inquiry has evaded theory or where the phenomenon's essence has yet to be adequately described (Ilsley and Krasemann, 2003). Given the rigors of phenomenology, it is advisable that the study ought to start with a subject of genuine interest to the researcher. In so being, as the researcher becomes attuned to the profundity of the experiences of others he also becomes attuned to his own (Cooper et al., 2000). Herein lies the obstacle. To ensure analytic integrity, the researcher must set aside preconceptions and presuppositions such that he is able to avoid unwittingly assigning his own meanings to another's experience (Ilsley and Krasemann, 2003). What follows is not meant to be a comprehensive look at the method guiding this study. That book has already been written. What is deserving of attention is the complexity of implementation given the particulars of this study. First: a little more background.

Unlike other modes of inquiry, a set formulaic process for phenomenological analysis has resisted universality. Part of the reason may lie in the fact that phenomenology is not only an interpretive research methodology, but also a school of thought, representing a diverse range of adherents (Ilsley and Krasemann, 2003). Despite disagreements as to what phenomenology is or is not, straightforward approaches to phenomenological inquiry exist nonetheless. A good example is Spiegelberg's (1965) three-step phenomenological exercise consisting of intuiting, analyzing, and describing. The first step calls for mindful and instinctual immersion in the experience or recollection of a given phenomenon. The second involves an exhaustive examination of the phenomenon from both outward (what is tangible and what has transpired) and inward (what is thought and what is felt) perspectives. The final step offers a description in which the process of intuiting (or sensing) and analyzing is documented and written as though the audience has never before experienced the phenomenon.

Historically, because of the contrast to more traditional and widely accepted objectivistic methods of inquiry, any findings born of interpretive methods have been prone to arouse greater levels of skepticism. Consequently, the credibility of any such study must surely rest with the level of authenticity the qualitative researcher is able to demonstrate. Perhaps surprisingly, whether or not one is convinced of the inherent strength of a given methodology is not necessarily a problem limited to the outside observer. Estranged from the method guiding his own doctoral research, Seidman's (1998) reaction upon discovery of phenomenological interviewing was visceral. Thereafter, he stated his belief that a case could be made for phenomenological interviewing as the most appropriate investigative method for some research situations, not the least of which was adult education. Having observed what must appear obvious, that the individual is most intimately aware of the history behind his intentional pursuits, Stanage (1987) identified the in-depth interview as especially well-suited to understand the meanings embedded within a person's unique set of educational experiences.

It must be noted that the in-depth interview differs significantly from interviews conducted for reasons other than research. Once the interview phase has been completed, the phenomenologist understands that there remains much to be learned. For example, although interviewees are asked to assign meanings to their experiences, it is with no certainty that their interpretations will withstand scrutiny. Whereas learning how each understands his engagement with the phenomenon is a vital component of the process, it is but one piece of the phenomenological puzzle—a puzzle that is solved only when the phenomenon's essence is made known. To assume that the interviewee is able to accurately recall his mental state at the time of an experience may be a careless mistake on behalf of the researcher. Quite simply, memory is not foolproof. No matter how certain someone may appear regarding his personal observation of a past psychological state, given the lack of a reliable way to assure accuracy, such observances cannot be considered a bias-free conduit to self-knowledge (Thomasson, 2005).

Just as the researcher must entertain the possibility that the interviewee's perceptions of an event may have dimmed (or outright changed) over time, he must avoid flavoring the interviewee's understandings via his own experiential filter (the collective set of experiences unique to an individual that helps or hinders his ability to make sense of the unfamiliar). This is where the phenomenological construct of bracketing comes in. Creswell (1997) defined bracketing as the process whereby a phenomenological researcher deliberately attempts to separate the phenomena in question from all previous understandings of it. The strength of bracketing is that it allows the researcher to examine a subject absent virtually all real-world constraints. It is not sufficient, however, for someone to simply claim such ability. To be credible, he must be able to demonstrate it. To be sure, bracketing is no simple task, as our human ability to make sense of new information rests upon previously established frameworks acquired through prior learning (Mezirow, 1991). Not only must the phenomenologist uncover his assumptions and hold them in check, he must acknowledge then contend with the fact that given a healthy mind, the experiential framework is an unavoidable reality. Knowing how it operates, however, can reduce the influential power of its filters.

My first major struggle with experiential filters involved having to suspend the assumption that my central research question was of absolute importance to my research. Phenomenology does not permit such rigidity. That my research question experienced numerous revisions between its inception and the completion of my dissertation suggests to me that I was successful in dodging the lure of assigning too much authority to a single presumption.

It is the public exploration of one's experiential framework and subsequent filters, that provides the researcher with what may be the best opportunity to convince the reader of a satisfactory—even admirable—level of transparency. Examination of one's own experience may also help the researcher to achieve greater intrapersonal transparency: a state of being whereby the person demonstrates an inner awareness and understanding (Armstrong, 1994). Thus equipped, such a person would have greater insight into the ways in which deeply held notions could otherwise magnify or dilute the conviction of one's conclusions.

Having set aside preconceptions (to the extent possible), the researcher must read the transcripts for statements of significance, trusting his ability to determine which statements are significant and which are not. To get this right, each transcript must be considered as a separate entity, unrelated to anything else. It is also important, during this stage, to avoid assigning greater value to one statement of significance over another. To do otherwise could serve to impose meaning rather than reveal it. To minimize imposition of ideas from one series of interviews to the next, Seidman (1998) reported a personal preference for completing all interviews before initiating any study of the transcripts. Next, repetitious material is removed and the remaining statements are clustered according to theme—which may be used in the construction of a narrative. Although creating thematically based narratives may be more conventional than constructing individual profiles, the profile can serve as an effective means to open an individual's experience to analysis. Despite its apparent value, however, the profile cannot serve as a substitute for inter-subject thematic analysis, which ultimately provides the means to answer the question, "What is the essence of this phenomenon?" Lastly, much like a postscript, the phenomenologist ponders any personal meanings he has drawn from having completed the research.

The Need for an Autobiographical Profile

It is paramount to phenomenology that the researcher be able to avoid approaching his inquiry without first having suspended personal bias. It would be reasonable to assume that the greater familiarity a researcher has with his subject of inquiry the greater the opportunity for bias to gain a foothold. To avoid such a misstep, the phenomenologist must cautiously approach the subject and stop short of the point where bias can no longer be assuredly suspended. Certainly, the more intimate the relationship between the phenomena and the phenomenologist, the more rigors would be necessary. In agreement with Schultz (2002) is my belief that given the right set of constructs (in addition to raw ability) it is quite possible to be immersed within a given subject and yet be able to suspend one's bias pertaining to it. For the reader to reach a similar level of confidence the researcher must be able to demonstrate not only a vested commitment to investigative integrity, but also the ability to follow through. Transparency is the key. Prefacing one's position with an autobiographic profile is one way to provide the reader with an evaluative point of reference.

From the researcher's perspective, the autobiographical profile has unspoken advantages, both literal and figurative. In contrast to the informant-interviewee, the researcher-autobiographer is not reliant solely upon the strength of verbal expression or limited by a non-negotiable period. If unhappy with a passage, the autobiographer has the latitude to remove it, a freedom disallowed a subject whose words have been recorded and frozen in time. As an exercise in phenomenology, however, it is vital to recognize this seeming advantage for the obstacle it can easily become. Being the autobiographer in question, without a dependable structure in place to keep my thoughts in check the more self-knowledge I have (or believe I have) the more I may be seduced into portraying an understanding of myself cultivated over time. Rather than construct an autobiographical profile with which I am already familiar, or would like to be identified by, I must find a way to separate my own set of experiences and thoughts from previously assigned meanings, both specific and generalized. To achieve my phenomenological objective, I must also proceed in such a way as to convince the reader of my impartiality. Paradoxically, the meanings I have assigned to my past experience (as well as to any number of reflections upon them) are inextricably interwoven with perceptions I have held, perceptions I currently hold, and perceptions in development or transition.

Autobiographic material was drawn from a number of sources, including: audio recordings of my dissertation committee meetings as well as my practice interview. As for its actual construction, I waited until after I had completed all four of the informant profiles as well as my investigation and analysis of thematic connections. In this way, any patterns that arose naturally from the data were able to shape the process without the lure of conformity pulling in some preconceived direction. Although I was mindful to keep my self-explorations largely consistent with those of the informants, I had the advantage of being able to assign meaning as I wrote. Then again, my profile is not, and was never intended to be, a source of data.

To what extent I am able to convince the reader of my aptitude, I do not know. What I do know is that any value resulting from this study is largely dependent upon the readers' conviction that, despite sharing an extraordinarily similar set of circumstances with the informants, I have been successful in demonstrating my integrity as a researcher through my commitment to the phenomenological method.

Notes on the Research Process

Having established the (initial) central question, I had to establish criteria for participatory consideration. The following was determined. All informants must have been diagnosed with Attention-Deficit/Hyperactivity Disorder (inattentive or combined type) in adulthood and be graduate students currently enrolled in an accredited adult education program. The Internal Review Board (IRB) at Northern Illinois University strongly advised that I accept self-reported diagnoses, insinuating that the bureaucracy involved in obtaining psychiatric diagnoses could be overwhelming.

In response to the dilemma of how many informants would be required, Seidman (1998) offered two criteria. The first addressed sufficiency, in which the researcher must ask whether the number of informants reflects the range one would expect to find at the site in question. The second addressed saturation of information, in which the researcher must identify the point at which no new significant information is likely to emerge. Although he cautioned that it is better to err on the side of too many informants, he also acknowledged that numerous factors (such as the geographic proximity of informant to researcher) do play a determining role. Accordingly (with approval of the IRB), I set the minimum number of persons necessary to continue my research at three, but remained open to the possibility of adding more. As for saturation, within minutes of initiating the first interview with my first informant, I began to feel the pangs of familiarity: feelings that would broaden and intensify as I completed subsequent interviews. Through the course of data collection (a period that lasted more than one year), four possible informants were ultimately rejected on a variety of grounds. All acceptable informants willingly signed an informed consent release ensuring the concealment of their identities. Each was assigned a pseudonym and all site-specific references were struck from the record.

My chosen method required each informant to be interviewed three times. Each interview would last ninety minutes. All three were to be completed within about two weeks time. During the first interview, the informant would describe personal experiences relevant to the subject, starting with early memories and on through the present. Questions were to be phrased to seek the "what" rather than the "why." During the second interview, the informant would describe current experiences with the phenomena. Both interviews sought concrete examples only, as personal meaning-making was reserved for the third and final interview. At the start of each interview, I read a brief statement to explain the purpose and scope of the specific interview (first, second, or third) being conducted. Also, in order to avoid leading any of the interviews and thus increasing the danger of implanting my own assumptions for discovery later on, I chose to read the central question at the start of each interview, curtailing any further explanation.

Once a series was complete, transcriptions were to be made from taped audio recordings of the interviews. After describing the arduous commitment necessary to prepare transcriptions, Seidman (1998) suggested that the researcher ought to consider hiring a transcriber. He referred to this as the ideal. Given my personal connection to the subject, however, I felt strongly that I needed to complete each step of the process myself. Accordingly, I identified pauses, changes in tonality, cadence and volume, as well as any reliance on gestures that I was able to recall. To all other incidentals (such as interruptions, laughter, or lapses of concentration) I gave equal attention.

Well before I began the process of selecting which passages to keep and which to discard, I decided to introduce the informants using biographic profiles. I saw this as a good way to establish a shared context, as each would have their stories presented according to a uniform set of life stages. I also felt that profiles might be more interesting, and at the same time, allow the reader to make observations apart from my own. Once all the transcriptions were reduced to statements of significance, they underwent a second evaluative phase. This time, I sought to identify only the most compelling among them. I constructed the profiles from this refined set. Never once did I move on to a subsequent phase for an informant before completing the present phase for each. After having fashioned coherent narratives, I corrected those elements common in speech that one would typically avoid in writing—such as stutters or verbal crutches. In addition to letting the profiles speak directly to the reader, I identified and explored issues within individual profiles as well as the themes I found woven throughout.

4

WHERE I HAVE BEEN AND WHO I MAY YET BECOME

The structure of the phenomenological interview helps to guide informants in the reconstruction of experience-based memories of the phenomena in question. Through the crafting of profiles, these collected reconstructions are packaged into an accessible and coherent format. Moreover, by relying on the informant's own words, the reader has conceptual access to the informant's consciousness at the time of the interview.

Understanding the profile to serve as a constructed point of reference for thematic connections to follow, I found limited editing to be both necessary and appropriate. I took painstaking effort so as not to jeopardize the intent of the informants' wording. [It was upon transcription of my own interviews that I realized how easily a message could be lost.] The challenge here was to maintain intent while avoiding obfuscation. Left unaltered were any incidence of contractions commonly used in speech. My feeling was that to do otherwise would have sapped some of the authenticity of having been a dialogue and not a correspondence.

Whereas the biographic profiles must contain sufficient data for the reader to assess the strength of my conclusions, my autobiographic profile served a somewhat different purpose. Lacking any intention to analyze my profile in light of the central question, there was no reason to present it as anything other than an uninterrupted narrative. Had I presented the informant profiles similarly, their power to illuminate would have been less. Consequently, they have been broken into contextually appropriate, congruent segments, each one prefaced with a brief introduction. [The first of the informant profiles appears in the next chapter.]

Autobiographic Learning Profile

In addition to having been diagnosed with Attention-Deficit/Hyperactivity Disorder (combined type), I have also been diagnosed with Obsessive-Compulsive Disorder (OCD). I learned of my AD/HD in my early thirties and my OCD a few years later. That was about a decade ago. Although any impact of OCD on my ability to learn is not specifically addressed here, each disorder has, at times, complicated the other. Then again, this is who I have always been and who I assume I always will be.

It was in the eighth grade that I recall having first thought about who I was as a learner. After completing a morning's worth of standardized tests, I was left with a feeling that the tests had somehow failed me. It was as though the questions had been written for someone else—that no matter how well or how poorly I did, the results would never be able to capture my true ability. In truth, I had had numerous social difficulties throughout childhood—thanks largely to an inability to decipher the social cues of my age group. When it came to academics, however, I generally did well. Perhaps predictably, given my age, I had already decided that my differences (with the exception of the recognition I received as an artist) were bad differences. I recall that things made sense for a short time after those tests and I wondered if just maybe, my whole way of thinking was somehow different from the norm. By the time high school began, however, my big moment of clarity had come and gone.

There I became aware of what I have since termed "gaps" in my ability to grasp certain types of concepts or to solve specific kinds of problems. Subjects such as algebra and chemistry, where we learned that some things were simply true regardless of whether or not they made any sense became sources of great anxiety. Most of my attempts to have things explained in a way that I could understand were met with replays of previous explanations. (Then again, I suspect I was not especially skilled at pinpointing or conveying my needs.) "Intentionally difficult," is a refrain I recall having been used to describe my school performance from an early age. Illustrative of how confusion could lead quickly to "intentionally difficult" was when, in chemistry class, we had to solve story-problems by multiplying various embedded numbers by some curious unit of measurement called a mole. Far more interested in sketching tiny rodents in the margins of my notebook and showing them to my classmates than facing the front of the room, I still managed to earn a grade of "C." The only applicable lesson I recall having learned in chemistry class was the importance of having a lab partner who understood the material. [Thanks again, Kevin.]

Even having discovered that I was nearsighted and having been fitted for glasses partway through the semester did not lead to improved understanding. Much of the time—then as now—I would approach problems holistically by immersing myself in a situation, whether real or theoretical, and waiting for solutions to emerge—at times with little conscious effort. This style of problem solving proved especially productive when the puzzle pieces made sense and where opportunities for movement and creativity were not deliberately expunged. When the pieces did not make sense or when the environment felt constrained, this epiphany-reliant approach would give way to strict linear-thinking. Much like a series of planks attached to a rope bridge, as each piece of information was added to the existing structure, I would progress only to the extent that the next piece of information made sense (both independent of, and dependent on, the whole). To engage a process that I could not fully understand would have been like trusting my full body weight to a theoretical plank.

Though I avoided foreign language and trigonometry, my curriculum was clearly top tier. Yet, once in the classroom, inflexibility often kept me from excelling. Certainly, having had a low threshold for frustration was no asset. Lacking the wherewithal to describe the particulars behind this wide-reaching phenomenon known now to be AD/HD (not to mention, OCD), I increasingly directed my frustrations inward. Although well aware that I possessed both intelligence and ability, I often felt maddened by my inability to channel them with consistency. Moreover, I allowed the talents I did possess to be overshadowed by perceptions of inadequacy. Despite involvement in cross-country, track, the school paper, and the fledgling photography club—all reasonably social activities—my poor self-image was compounded by a general mystification with social norms. At school I played to my status as somewhat of an eccentric goofball. In private, I would beat myself up for the very same.

For some reason, it never occurred to me that in order to attend college, I had to apply for college. This disorganized sense of things continued through one year of community college, a near-fatal car accident (including five months fastened into a neck and back brace) and into Northern Illinois University as a sophomore, where the concept of having to declare a major caught me by surprise. Energized by my transition into adulthood, yet unable to shake off my doldrums I rightly decided to seek counseling—a decision I would repeat several times in subsequent years. During my second counseling experience of adulthood, I became interested in observing myself from a third-person perspective, asking myself the sort of questions a counselor might ask. After graduating with a Bachelor of Fine Arts degree (mainly because creating art was comforting) and lacking any real job options, I managed to be hired as an occupational therapy technician in the adult psychiatric wing of a local hospital. This unexpected event introduced me to the care provider side of mental health services. With the exception of a two-year hiatus, I have worked in this area ever since.

After several years of low pay and a sense of professional aimlessness, I decided to seek a master's degree. I considered social work, computer animation, and fine art. Ultimately, I picked a program in outdoor teacher education. Quite simply, my parents were professors within the program, and what they did for a living looked good to me. Yet, following acceptance, it took nearly two years for me to register for my first class. It should have been obvious that my decision lacked clarity. I never saw it. Worse, after a year and a half of classes I had no idea of what I would do upon graduation. Conveniently, a graduate assistant quit suddenly and I was offered the balance of her assistantship. Although I had brazenly quit my job as a residential childcare worker, quickly liquidated my savings and began taking out student loans, the assistantship provided me with a real sense of what having the degree might mean. Even better, the program welcomed all learning styles. Seventeen years after having recognized (and quickly forgotten) the disconnection I felt with regard to standardized tests, I recalled the eighth grade insight. I also recalled an important experience I had as an undergraduate art student.

The first assignment of my second painting class began with random application of paint to canvas. After a few days of manipulating oil paint into meaningless swirls, blotches, and globs we were instructed to put away our brushes and to study our nonrepresentational pieces to determine what was and what was not working. Thereafter, we were to fix any problems we encountered. Huh? On my own, I have been more-or-less successful at creating thought-provoking images, but in that studio—I was not on my own. Ominously between my stretched canvas and my way forward was the confounding vision of an unwaveringly serious man. Never before had I encountered so many gaps in the same place at the same time. After several days of grimacing, I was saved by the realization that the product was as meaningless as the process of abstract problem solving was meaningful. Unfortunately, I lacked the philosophic framework to fully capitalize on the insight. Like others before, this epiphany momentarily reared itself then disappeared. Had I not become immersed in the culture of outdoor experiential education—where abstract problems seemed to lie in wait beneath every stone and beyond every swale—it likely would have vanished altogether. Rather, I came to understand that it was possible to consider—even solve—problems that lacked clear definition. Wherever I found a gap, I merely had to fill it with a question, which in turn would establish a direction. As I would discover years later, this process of *problem-posing* was a crucial step in critical thought.

Convinced that I was on the threshold of a breakthrough in self-understanding, I decided the time was right to seek an advanced degree. Given that I had not put much thought into what I would do upon graduation, I also saw my continued education as a safe haven. [Safe from what? Probably, from having to make the sort of real-world decisions I often found so daunting.] Proximity (as usual) played the most influential role in choosing a program (as I have always resisted moving more than several hour's drive from my parents). I knew that I would stay with education, but since I had no idea of where a doctoral degree in education might lead, I had a tough time picking just the right one. On little more than an acquaintance's suggestion, I decided to apply to a program in adult education. Impulsiveness (it should be noted) is an oft-cited issue for individuals diagnosed with AD/HD. Many times, I have stood staring up at fast food menus, unable to select which variation of burger and fries to purchase. I have wasted entire afternoons simply trying to decide how best to spend my time. Conversely, when it has come to choices of monumental proportions, my typical response has been to make some abrupt, poorly considered decision and plow ahead, full force.

Having thus stepped onto the envisioned doctoral threshold, a second (potentially, life-altering) decision leapt into the mix. For reasons I was unable to explain, I had decided to concurrently fulfill a long-standing dream of earning a Master's of Fine Arts degree in painting. When the professorate of each program questioned my reasoning, I had nothing to offer but a confounding sense of urgency. This time I recognized the absurdity of my plan. Four years after my previous counseling experience had ended, the time had come for another round. A few weeks later, I dropped out of the painting program.

During my tenth counseling session, my counselor asked what I knew about AD/HD. Although I had spent two years working with mentally ill adults and almost four years with emotionally disturbed boys (many of whom had AD/HD), I did not know much. The results of my first test for AD/HD were inconclusive. Yet, I became captivated with the possibility. I began reading on the subject and the more I read, the more I became convinced that AD/HD is exactly what I had. The books also provided a sense of community. Yet, whenever an author offered some suggestion for coping I would lose interest. Having been able to come so far without someone else's advice (counseling notwithstanding) was a source of stubborn pride that I was not about to dilute. Even had pride not been an issue, I doubt I would have given any technique the time required to master it.

Shortly thereafter, I enrolled in the course that would have the greatest direct impact on my ability to understand myself in terms of who I was as a learner. The course was titled: *Learning How to Learn*. The concepts and techniques were at once simple and powerful. We were instructed to keep a learning journal and to make a habit of observing ourselves as we engaged in learning activities. Although I experimented with some of this as a master's student, my efforts had been inconsistent. Gibbons' (1990) working model of the Learning-How-to-Learn process greatly impressed me with its ease of application. Its central tenets of awareness, self-monitoring, and reflection provided a strategy that I could easily put to work in situations where I typically struggled to concentrate or contribute. The following details a series of discoveries made during experimentation with self-regulated learning.

I had been a copious note-taker for years, but seldom gave them more than a glance once the class was over. Given renewed curiosity and a dependable structure for observation, I decided to explore the role of note-taking in my studies. My first discovery was that the physical act of writing helped me to maintain focus. Interestingly, when my level of anxiety rose during a class, so long as I took faster notes, I was able to keep the anxiety in check. Furthermore, I discovered that it was not even necessary to take notes on whatever the presenter was saying. During an interesting, yet anxiety-inducing course on worker movements within adult education, I decided to take notes on the anxiety I felt sure to experience. Throughout much of the session, I furiously penned my moment-to-moment experience. At the time, I had no idea what insight, if any, the experiment might yield. It would seem that by taking notes on an entirely different subject, whatever had been discussed in class should have been a mental wash. Instead, I was surprised at how well I understood the material. Through further observation, I have found that this strategy is effective only in circumstances where I experience a high degree of anxiety. For a time, such personal discoveries became commonplace, as I directed increasing levels of awareness to my total participation in learning situations. Self-awareness would uncover what was and was not working, while abstract problem-solving skills allowed me to devise corrective actions in real-time.

Perhaps one benefit of frenetic note taking is that I am allowed a great deal of physical movement (albeit within a very limited range). Similar to the doodling and chair-rocking that kept me occupied and seated through much of grade school, I found that repetitive hand, finger, leg, and/or foot motion has helped me to alleviate some amount of stress—thus enabling greater concentration. When given access to full-range motion, however, the benefits are much more pronounced. I found that I was much less likely to become distracted during a good walk where I could talk aloud than had I been sitting inside of a classroom; walking while talking availed a reservoir for clarity that was otherwise largely unavailable.

After completing most of my adult education classes, I could no longer avoid the comprehensive exam that was necessary to officially be cast as a doctoral candidate. As a means to secure a private testing room through the campus Office of Resource Accessibility—an example of a nondiscriminatory accommodation for individuals with disabilities (Richard, 1995b)—I sought formal diagnosis. In addition to being given my own room, free from outside distractions, I was allowed a time extension. For the first time during an exam, I was able to get up and walk around. I jumped up and down. I paced. I fiddled with things, made noises, sang aloud and talked to myself. It felt liberating. Had I been in a setting where someone else was tapping a pencil (for example), my ability to concentrate would have been compromised. Much worse are instructors who interrupt an exam in order to impart some last-minute scrap of wisdom. Following a single interruption, I might silently curse to myself. A few more interruptions and I might enter a silent rage. Being unable to control the testing environment often evoked a sense of being trapped. Whether trapped literally (such as having an instructor who rambles on after class has technically ended) or conceptually (such as having an idea that I cannot bring to fruition) I have often experienced a spike in my level of anxiety. In response I typically would begin rocking, bouncing on my toes or pacing when upright, sighing, and/or twitching my fingers in rapid semi-predictable patterns.

The inescapable reality of having to read numerous and oftentimes dry articles and texts as part of my doctoral studies led to the development of a very workable, multi-stage compensatory strategy. Before starting medications, I was never much of a reader. I considered a book on multiple intelligence theory to be one of the most influential that I "read" during my masters program, yet I never even made it to the end of the first chapter. I also experienced other reading-related obstacles. Suppose that I had chapters from two different textbooks to read sometime during the week. Each time I would pick up one book, I found that two things were very likely to happen. Unless the text was truly captivating, my mind nearly always drifted off. Much like a person may arrive at a destination and only vaguely recall the drive, I would periodically find myself on some page and have no recollection of what I had presumably read. At other times, even upon extending considerable effort to remain focused, I found that by the time I got to the end of a sentence I could scarcely recall how the sentence began. This was old news. It was the discovery of the second obstacle that caught me by surprise.

Once I decided which book to read and actually began reading, I would experience a strong sense that I ought to be reading the other book. If I were to switch to the second book, I would suddenly experience the same feelings about the first. At other times, when able to stay with a single book, I would force myself to start on the very first page, even if the information I sought appeared elsewhere. Simply turning to the page containing the information was out of the question. A good example of an absurd situation masquerading as normal, this self-assigned rule frequently kept me from ever making it to the pages of interest. The resulting frustration was immense, yet by then I had convinced myself that any violation of the rule would be a confirmation of my inadequacy as a serious student. Assuming that such rigidity most likely stemmed from my dual disorders did nothing to alleviate the need to follow strict internal rules, no matter how blatantly unproductive—even bizarre. Complicating any effort to sit down and read were all kinds of little noises and extraneous thoughts that would continuously vie for my attention. Six months before I took the candidacy exam, I decided that I needed a workable compensatory learning strategy. By this time, I was aware that the majority of strategies I had come to consciously rely on began with self-observation. I took notice of what seemed to be working in certain situations and cultivated that which worked the best. This would be my first attempt to design a strategy from scratch.

The result worked surprisingly well. Although an unpleasant experience overall, it provided a sense of real accomplishment. I had sixteen texts with which to become familiar. The first step was to create an order. Before I picked up a book, I already knew which book would be next, and so on through all sixteen. Each time I settled down to read, I would assign myself ten pages—all to be read without a break. Hungry? Thirsty? Need to use the washroom? Too bad. Sorry. No way. I had to complete the assigned pages before doing anything else. At the end of each segment, however, I allowed a measure of flexibility. I could assign another ten pages, or I could take a break. As I read, I would highlight those passages that were of interest or seemed to be of value. As I did, I made no attempt to remember anything. Rather, my goal was to remain on task and in the present at all times. Upon completing a book, I would type all of the highlighted passages and their corresponding page numbers into my computer. This system generally served to condense a book by about ninety percent. It was this condensed version that I would read for comprehension. When it became necessary to flesh out a concept or check a passage for accuracy, I would use the page citations to reference the original text. The strategy worked wonderfully. Even now that I take medications, it has remained useful.

Another magnet for the interplay of symptoms, old habits, and new strategies has been my relationship with procrastination. As far back as I can remember I nearly always waited to start assignments and projects until just before the last possible minute. From cleaning my room as a child to finishing up revisions to this book, I have always wasted a lot of time. During my undergraduate years it dawned on me that no matter how much I procrastinated, I was nearly always able to complete my assignments on time. Of course the more enjoyable the activity, the less procrastination would be an issue. Even given the remarkable differences made possible through medications, I still have to take the pills before I can receive the benefit. And unless I take them shortly after I wake, the thought of having to return to my closet, reach up, take out the pills, and swallow them by sticking my head into the bathroom sink is enough to postpone that minor (yet significant) task for hours.

Sometime after completing the course, *Learning How to Learn*, I became aware of periodic episodes of clarity similar to what I now experience twenty minutes or so after ingesting my morning medications. I suspect that these moments have likely occurred throughout my life. Similar to the way in which anxiety-induced drive has proven reliable, so long as I began working shortly after the clarity was first felt, anxiety-free momentum would carry me through. If I waited too long, however, the clarity would pass and with it the chance to complete my task nearly symptom free. Despite serious effort, I have never been able to anticipate these periods.

Amidst all the unseen obstacles encountered while navigating a lifetime's worth of learning experiences as a person with AD/HD, the process of writing a research proposal and having it approved was perhaps the most frustrating experience of my student life. In January of 2001, I began a class designed to help students to write their dissertation proposals. That May, we took turns presenting our proposals to the class. The experience left me energized and I recall wanting to run out and start collecting data. What I failed to realize was that a punishing, yet necessary, tradition of weeding out all but the most resilient candidates was about to be unleashed. For me, this tradition would play out over the next two and one half years.

As it happened, the first meeting with my dissertation committee took place on September 11, 2001. Suddenly critical self-examination, compensatory learning styles, AD/HD and the rest did not seem so important. In their place I felt alarm at the extent to which our government was apparently blindsided. This was followed by a sense of unease that the administration seemed to be capitalizing on what had been a monumental security failure. After spending years of my life studying the ways in which adults learned, I was genuinely troubled to see the citizenry's collective curiosity be so overwhelmingly dampened by a rise of nationalism. The attacks on September 11, 2001 proved to be a transformative learning experience for me—defined by Mezirow (1991) as a process whereby a person reinterprets an experience using a new set of expectations, thus assigning a new meaning to an old experience. The question occupying my mind was no longer, "Who am I as a learner?" It was, "What is really going on in the world and what decisions, policies, and actions are behind whatever is happening?" Perhaps it was even more basic than that. I wanted to know who *we* had become as Americans—and why.

Given my poor record of completing books (including those of interest), the speed at which I was able to acquire a working knowledge of modern history was plodding. Once I began taking medications to treat my AD/HD, however, I found that I was able to read nearly anything I wanted with considerable ease. As consequence, time that could have easily been spent dedicated to academic progress was given to matters of policy, opinion, and national and world affairs.

At irregular intervals, I made progress nonetheless. Eventually a single, seemingly insurmountable barrier remained: I had yet to choose a method. Although I had a strong vision as to how to proceed, I had considerable trouble convincing my committee of the same. While transcribing the taped recording of the committee meeting in which I expressed my frustrations, I noticed something. Up to the point where I began to bemoan my fortune, I spoke with reasonable lucidity. Suddenly my cadence became a rapid string of words and sentence fragments thrown together. My voice twisted with emotion and projected a sense of bewildered energy. Whereas the program itself had been liberating, the proposal process seemed a maze of red tape and a hodge-podge of baffling expectations. Following my proposal's eventual approval—captured on the same tape—I regained a sense of calm. During the transcription process, I began to reflect on the experience. From what had been a confusing swirl of emotion, I was able to identify five primary reasons for the long delay.

The first involved getting three college professors together in the same place at the same time. As only face-to-face meetings were allowed, whenever one of the members was on vacation, on sabbatical, or had any other scheduling conflict, a joint meeting could not take place. Such conflicts ate up months at a time. The second concerned the fact that it took so long for me to find the exact method of inquiry. Perhaps taking the idea of student-centered learning too far, I wasted a lot of time attempting to convince my committee that I could invent my own method as I went. Although I knew how I wanted to proceed in a general sense, until I could state my methodological approach with certainty, my proposal was stuck. The third obstacle was difficult to recognize. Once I did, however, it was with renewed regard for the professorate. Thanks to my own defensiveness, what seemed at the time to range from squabbles over minor details to an underlying lack of regard for my capabilities was (as I now understand it) a tactic to test my resolve. Without an unwavering sense of purpose, it was likely that anything I wrote would be substandard (if able to complete the research at all). The fourth obstacle was deeply personal. During the autumn of 2001, on the first day of my new administrative position as an adult educator, I became a first-time father. In addition to my increased responsibility at home, every thing in my life shifted in loving accommodation of my son. The final conflict resided at the aforementioned intersection of my increased interest in politics and world affairs and the decision to treat my AD/HD with medication.

With a clear mind and absent any day-to-day distractions, nearly any type of political information was now only a few clicks away on the Internet. Being able to pursue knowledge free from institutional constraints inherent within the university system made this the biggest distraction of all. Once I began the transcription process, however, I felt a renewed sense of ownership and was able to fight off what had become a deeply rooted and wide-ranging distraction. It was not until I had nearly completed this autobiographical profile that I truly understood what must have been obvious to those close to me. Despite all my self-knowledge and all the benefits of medication, I still had AD/HD.

5

MARIANNE:
"I got the idea that you never quit."

At the time of our first interview, Marianne was a fifty-year old doctoral student. She was diagnosed with AD/HD at age forty-two. Each of our interviews took place midday in February of 2004, at one of her university's branch campuses. One difficulty of my interviews with Marianne was that she had a soft, lilting voice that would trail away at times, resulting in my periodic inability to fully transcribe her recorded words.

Experiences of Youth

Despite the accommodations her way of being and knowing required, as well as the efforts she took to address them, Marianne perceived her situation without alarm. Arguably, the lack of early criticism and her avoidance of the teaching staff served to limit opportunities for negative self-perceptions to form. [Marianne's narrative begins.]

I always went to parochial schools where the class size was small, structured, and didn't offer a whole lot of freedom. In elementary school, classes were run pretty much on fear. The nuns were like gods and you did everything you could to stay out of trouble. Otherwise, there would be heck to pay when you got home. I think that saved me. I suspect if I hadn't gone to a Catholic school I would have been in all kinds of trouble. I was a really poor decision-maker and a big risk-taker. I would do stupid stuff if I didn't have people watching me, but in class, I was quiet. I didn't bother anyone but my head was always in a different place thinking about books that I had read or just looking out the window. I never thought about this before, but when I'd look out the window I always wondered about people and things. I would wonder who that was, where they lived, what they liked to do, where they got those clothes. Just on and on. Those are the same kinds of things that I've probably done my whole life. I could sit in an airport for hours and just watch people go by. I'd wonder what he does. I'd wonder what makes him buy clothes like that. I'd wonder what he was thinking. Things like that.

In fourth grade, I just lost math. But my grades were good enough that it didn't frighten me into thinking that something was wrong. I just thought that's the way it was. Later on, as a high school student, I barely made it through algebra. It didn't connect at all. I just never saw it. I could do a chapter test as long as it wasn't asking me to synthesize or discriminate. I could do that. But when you combined a number of types of problems, I couldn't get it. Back then we didn't talk about study skills and study strategies. You pretty much went to class and did your best. It wasn't like somebody would ever call you out into the hall and say you did a really nice job. And with math, I really needed to do it by myself because it took so much concentration and repetition and talking it through aloud that I couldn't work with anybody. It took me so long to get those concepts that when I did try to work with other people, they were always way ahead of me and I would have no idea what they were talking about. But I had good writing skills in high school even though we were just doing paragraphs without a lot of room for creativity. Nuns are not big on creativity. I just thought that some people are unbalanced. I'm good at English but I'm not good at math. That's just the way some people are.

I also became a really good note-taker in high school. Now that I think about it, I realize that the only way I could stay on task was to write down whatever the instructor was saying. It was a very competitive high school and grades were something I really wanted. At that age it's very important to be accepted and people who didn't get good grades were not. When ninety percent of your class goes to college, including places like Harvard, it becomes very important for you to do things like that. So I did. I guess the note taking was a strategy I came up with. Another was to highlight the text and take notes that would help me to remember so I wouldn't have to read the whole chapter over again. I still do this. People laugh at me. I highlight everything. I can't read without highlighting or I can't stay on task. It also helps me to remember where I was. I would lose track, go back, and say, "Well, I must have read this because I highlighted it." They were appropriate, though. It wasn't just random. I think the highlighting strategy just happened. I don't remember thinking I needed a strategy. It was fear of humiliation really, that pushed me.

Adulthood Experiences

Of particular interest concerning Marianne's early adulthood was the level of impulsivity she brought to major life decisions. Also noteworthy were the realizations she began to have.

During the summer after graduation, I met someone. I fell in love and I got married. I just decided that's what I was going to do. One day I said to my mom, "You know, I don't think I'm going to go to school after all. I think I'm just going to get married and start having a family." Her heart stopped beating. It just came out of nowhere. This was a person I knew for—I don't know—six—seven weeks. Hmm. My parents begged me to go to a community college, which I did. And it was so easy for me because I had been to that really competitive high school. It was the first time in my life that grades weren't important. I waited to get married until after I earned an associate degree.

I guess we waited about six or seven years to have kids and during that time, I had a lot of jobs that were boring. I had my first child when I was twenty-seven. Twenty-six? Twenty-seven. I had Keri when I was twenty-nine—I think. And when she started first grade, I returned to school. I always thought that I'd go into education, even back in high school. I just didn't know what I would teach. Then I learned about a friend's nephew who had a learning disability. He could memorize anything, but had no understanding of what he was memorizing. Intrigued, I decided to study learning disabilities. I don't think my decision to become a teacher was gender-based. I've thought a lot about that. I was never pushed into traditional roles for females. I was always told that I could be whatever I wanted. I think it's just something I always thought that I was good at, so it was a choice that I probably would have made no matter what. That's how I was raised. There aren't any barriers unless you put them there. I've always been very privileged in terms of education. My family was very supportive.

When I started my bachelor's degree, I thought I would teach elementary school. Then as time passed, I felt this disconnect starting to happen. I called my local community college and asked if they were hiring any tutors. And you know what? They said they were. That just sort of came my way and wasn't anything I had ever planned on. When you go for job interviews and people ask where you see yourself in ten years—I've never been where I thought I would be. Even in five years. It just never worked for me.

At my new job, I taught a developmental math course that was sort of self-paced, and through it, I realized that there were all these tricks to math that allowed me to see things I couldn't see before. I discovered fraction kits, for example. The kits are very kinesthetic. You actually take felt and cut it into pieces. Then you take it apart and put it back together. It just made so much more sense to me than seeing it in a book. I thought, shoot! Where have I been? I realized there were chunks of math that I had just lost. Absolutely lost.

Point of Diagnosis

Helping lead to her diagnosis was Marianne's ability to recognize her own traits mirrored in her daughter's experiences. And although Marianne's drive for solutions strengthened her self-confidence, it also served to partially obstruct specific knowledge pertaining to her deficits.

My daughter and I were diagnosed together. I was learning more about ADD on my job and starting to look at my daughter and think, oh my God. This is what she looks like and this is what I look like. Keri would have been in first grade. She was always very fidgety. A lot of kids at that age are fidgety. It finally caught up with Keri her freshman year of high school. By that time, she was just daydreaming so much. As Keri talked about the things that were happening to her and how uncomfortable she was, it brought back a lot of memories about how I felt in high school. I realized that the things that she was describing that seemed normal to me were probably not normal. I thought that's the way you live. You just daydream and you get bored and you come back and you try to figure out what's going on. You would listen to what the instructor said and then just start thinking about something totally different. Then you would come back to realize that whole pieces of conversations were gone and someone was calling on you. Anyway, I'm fifty now, so that would have been in 1996? You know I'm going to be really stupid at math. I was born in 1953 and would have been diagnosed in 1996. Right? Yeah. I graduated in 2000. And freshman year would have been—shoot. That would have been 1996.

You know, I think I was focused so much more on getting my daughter straight and getting her comfortable with that diagnosis that I didn't notice it so much in myself—other than thinking: yeah, that explains that. You know? I think the noticeable difference for me didn't come with the diagnosis. It came when I went back to school to get my bachelor's degree. I was so much more focused. I just took it so much more seriously. Those strategies were always there, but as an adult student, I was so much more ready to be in school. I think going back to school, as an adult learner, you're making sacrifices. When you're taking time away from your family and other things, I think your motivation to do well is much stronger. And there were a lot of people who knew what I was doing and I guess that was motivation for me too. I was not going to quit no matter what. I don't know where that comes from: that you just don't quit. You never quit at anything no matter how hard it is. By that time, I already had pretty sufficient academic success. And again, I still had that thing that came from my parents. If I worked really hard I could do anything, and there wasn't anything that could stop me.

I don't have any objection to medications for ADD. I'm just not sure what the benefits would be for me. There's a lot that I've figured out. You choose jobs that will maximize your strengths and minimize your deficits, or minimize the things that you aren't as good at. And I think the jobs that I've had have always involved multitasking: doing a variety of different things and having different responsibilities. My job is never the same every day. I think if I didn't have that kind of job, the need for medication would be more pronounced. Does that make sense? Anyway, I have a very concrete, logical way of thinking. For me it's about the end product. Maybe it just comes back to not giving up. If I had a problem I needed to fix, I just figured out a way to do it. Sometimes I tend to jump to a solution because I get so much more satisfaction. I'm much more likely to say, "We discussed it. We're done. Here's the solution. Let's move on." Years later, when I read those ADD self-help books I thought: oh! This is in a book?

As for ways in which my diagnosis changed how I thought about myself, it was in terms of needing to be more aware whenever I felt myself getting angry. When you get into the workplace there's not as much forgiveness as there is within your family. There have been stupid things I've said and done out of impulsively and anger that I wish I hadn't.

Considering Adult Education

As driven for solutions as she had become, much of Marianne's self-knowledge pertained to what she would rather avoid. Although her career continued to progress, as her conflicts became more visible, they also became less deftly managed.

As part of my present job, I supervise some really bright, bright students. What an incredible experience that was. I had always worked with students who were struggling. To supervise students who excelled at everything was just incredible. For some reason it made me want to go back to school. I guess I saw the excitement that they had in learning and I missed that. I also knew that if I were going to go any place in higher education, I would have to be enrolled in a doctorate program.

There were a number of people on my campus who were getting their doctorates, including this cohort. Those people would be together in every single class throughout their whole program. Those people would have driven me crazy. There was no academic freedom, no choices, and seeing those same people for all those years—I don't think I could do that. Those people would just get on my nerves. I guess that goes back to flexibility. They're all taking the same classes. Although their dissertations will be very different, I think that their education should be different too. They all seem to be thinking the same way. They're all studying the same theorists and when they come back from class, all their opinions are the same. They have the same seriousness and the same dedication to learning as I do, but I just don't think they're getting the same thing out of it. They're not getting opportunities for discovery. They don't have any opportunities for diversity. And they're not seeing a broader picture. They're exploring, but within this very narrow field of vision.

I think part of my decision to study adult education has to do with boredom. I could have gone back to special education. I could have gone back to curriculum and instruction, but I felt like I had been there already. I felt like I had already done that and I wonder if other people in the program didn't choose adult education for that same reason. It was an opportunity to take a look at a whole new body of knowledge that I hadn't looked at before. I think one of the strengths of having ADD is that you do think creatively and you do see things from all different ways. I may not necessarily agree with one train of thought, but because I can see all different directions, I can find a way to bring things together. Not being stuck on that same train gives you the opportunity to take what you feel comfortable with and make it your own.

At work, there's this frustrating situation that involves the hierarchal way our organization is structured. If I have a question, I have a tendency to ask the person I know has the answer rather than asking the person directly above me who doesn't know the answer and who will have to ask somebody else who will have to ask the person I would have asked originally. My boss talks to her boss who talks to his boss and so it goes: over, down, back up, over, back down. I just can't deal with that, so I try to explain to my boss how frustrating it is for me. Then I start drawing pictures. It's the only way I can think to explain it to her. So even when those kinesthetic pieces to pick up and hold aren't there, I'm still trying to create my own, in a way. I think it's my preferred way of learning, which makes it hard to back away from. When I taught in a traditional classroom I was able to teach to everybody's learning style even though it made more sense to me, to explain it my way. I'm used to thinking if something needs to get done you find a way to do it. When there's a problem at work I'm much more likely to push people to go back and look at the problem again. If we have a problem and the solution we have in place is not working, the hierarchy will say, "We're going to make this work," whereas I'd be more likely to say, "It's not working. It's not going to work. Let's stop trying to jam that round peg into that square hole." A couple of months ago I had the opportunity to take a higher-level administrative position and I didn't do it because I knew that I could not attend all those meetings. In a large organization such as mine policy doesn't change very quickly. There seems to be a lot of discussion that leads nowhere and that's not one of my strengths.

I think that people I've worked with for a long time have just gotten used to the fact that I jump topics. Another bad habit I have is interrupting. As people are talking, I'm processing information so quickly, that I think I know what they're going to say and I'm already responding without having given them a chance to finish. Maybe that's one of the reasons why I'm having so much trouble concentrating today. Later, I'm headed to a meeting with a person who processes information very slowly, so there are large gaps while he's trying to get out what he's trying to say. And that's very frustrating for me. I want to say, "Come on!" To sit back and wait for him to finish is very hard. "Come on! Say it! I know what you're going to say! Do you want me to just say it for you?" Yeah, it's very frustrating for me when things don't work quickly. I think that's one of the struggles of supervising me. It's really hard to keep me to an agenda. It is like when I started this doctoral program I promised myself I would take one class at a time, which is just a joke because I think I did that once. And then I got impatient and said to myself, "You can do two. There's no reason why you can't do two. You have good study habits. You manage your time well. You can do two."

I'm not a front-rower either. I think a part of that is because I know I'm not going to be paying attention some of the time. If I'm going to be doing that I prefer to be doing that at the back, rather than directly in front of somebody. I think in the past I tried to sit in the front to see if that would help me pay attention and it really didn't. It just didn't matter if the person was right in front of me or not. I was still thinking about other things.

The Graduate School Experience

At this stage of Marianne's life, conflicts have been tempered by greater self-understanding and self-control. With increased cognizance of problem areas there has come a refined ability to strategize as well as to see the humor inherent in some missteps. Less likely to find herself at odds with others, Marianne has come to savor a deep respect for the diversity of her fellow learners.

This university has always been very good to me. I looked at a number of places, and none of them seemed to have the flexibility and the choices that we have. For the most part, you're kind of left alone, which is okay. I mean, when I want to see my chairperson I just email and ask when it's convenient, but I don't have the pressure of constantly doing it. I can be pretty obsessive about things like that, so I think she realized I put that kind of pressure on myself and that she doesn't really need to put any pressure on me.

When I first started this program one of the things that I was looking at is what make some people want to continue when others don't? Because when I tell people I'm in a doctoral program, for the most part they think I'm crazy. "Why are you doing that?" And "God, that's such a grind." And that's a question I've never had an answer to: What makes me keep doing it? I think as a learner I place really high expectations on myself. I think at this level the push has to come from within you and I don't know where that comes from. Is it something that you're just born with? Somewhere I got the idea that you never quit and quitting is a bad thing. Somehow, it's just part of how I'm wired. I get an incredible sense of accomplishment. And as I've matured over the years, I've learned not to expect people to share in that satisfaction. You have to be willing to do it for yourself and you can't expect people to provide you with constant reinforcement. I'm not going to get a lot of things like pats on the back for having three classes left. So as a learner I think I'm really driven.

When I talk to other people in doctoral programs, the concept of adult continuing education is very difficult for them to understand. It can cover so many different things. An accountant I work with thought it was a joke. He said, "You're not doing anything. The way you conduct your research is loose. There just isn't anything there. You're just getting a degree in anything." But I would ask him, "How can you sit there through all that accounting stuff? How can you sit through those courses over and over and over again? Yours is so rigid." To me, learning doesn't have to be painful. In adult education, we're interested in hearing other people's perspectives. That makes us different, I suppose. If we're teachers, we're looking to improve how we teach. We are asking, "How can we provide a better service to our students? How can we provide better education?"

I've never thought of this before, but recently the other two departmental deans and I had a talk about collaboration. The dean of computer information systems said, "I can tell you right now my people aren't going to want to collaborate. They really don't care what anybody else thinks." The business dean said, "Some of my people will. Some of my people won't." In general education, where I am the dean, and where most people are trained as teachers, everybody wants to collaborate. It's like this one course where we worked in teams and picked a project that was very creative and you know what? I have no idea what the topic was. I'm just going totally blank. I don't even know what my piece was. Anyway, the thing that I liked about this particular group is that we were willing to change roles. There was never a situation where somebody felt that they had to take control and be the leader or that they weren't willing to listen to what other people had to say. I've really been impressed that everyone is very serious about what they're doing. No matter where people are coming from, everybody takes it very seriously. And even though our backgrounds are very different, it's real easy for us to work together. I've had the opportunity to do a lot of things that I wanted to do and to take classes that I've wanted to take. I don't think there's anything that I've taken that I haven't wanted to.

When I first started this program, I used to hate driving out to the campus. Then in the critical thinking course that I took, we did so much reflection that I started looking forward to those trips. It was time to think and reflect. Once I got home, I would usually take the laptop into the bedroom, sit on the bed and just spread everything out. Then I would turn the TV on. My husband would come in and ask what I'm watching. Well, I wouldn't really be watching it. It is just noise. Sitting at a desk and spreading out papers in organized piles isn't something that I would do. When I'm sitting with all this stuff spread out all over, I know that everything I need is there. I've never been real comfortable sitting at a desk for a long period of time, so stretching out and not having to sit on a chair just seems better. Besides, when I am sitting at a desk I never seem to be able to find everything I'm looking for. I'd spend all day there. I just don't do that well sitting.

I also spend a lot of time talking to myself, talking aloud, reading papers aloud to make sure it's the way I want it to be. For some reason, vocalizing is really helpful to me. I find myself repeating things and often wonder why. Why am I doing that? Why do I keep saying that same thing over and over again? I'm not sure if it's because I need validation from the listener, that they understand. Or, is it because I've gone so far off that I need to come back and repeat it just to get myself back on track again? Oh, and I cannot study quietly. Going to the library is a good place for me now, but when I was younger, the library was one of the worst places because I'd just start distracting other people. It was so quiet that I couldn't stand it—so I'd start talking. In fact, I found myself doing that today, in a room just a little bit bigger than this. These two clerical people were in the room and as they were trying to concentrate, I'm there and I can't stop talking to them. I'm sure they were thinking: Okay, she's supposed to be here for another hour. How are we supposed to get anything done? She won't stop! I'm supposed to be a dean. I'm supposed to be a person in charge. I do stuff all the time that's wrong and I don't even realize it.

I recently took statistics and loved it. I always enjoyed doing research. The way the professor taught this class is the absolutely best way for me to learn. We had a text with a study guide that had all the things I needed to learn and understand, like the math. I could read the chapter ahead of time and the chapter wouldn't make any sense. I could do the study guide ahead of time and work backwards. Does that make sense? I would try to do problems in the study guide, then go back, and look for the answers. Rather than reading the text and trying to do the problem, I would try to do the problem then search for the solution in the text. That's a study skill I teach. It focuses your thinking and you actually end up reading the whole chapter. If you start with the chapter and read the whole thing, you don't really know what to focus on. And if you can't concentrate, it's hard for you to pick out what's important. I think I started doing it in high school: working backwards. I never realized that before. By the time we were ready to leave statistics each day, I was done. I was just done. Couldn't think. They'd say, "Let's stay and finish it." Well, I'd stay, but I can tell you I was of no use whatsoever. It's internal. Especially with material like that because I'm not good at math and even though I enjoyed it, there's a certain point where I just can't take it. I just can't take it anymore. I know I'll get it. I'm just not going to get it then. I'm somewhere else: thinking about other things, making lists. I'm a big list maker. Once I shut down, I start thinking about other things I need to do. I can't take in any more of that kind of information. A piece of it is boredom. I need a new game. I don't want to play this one. I want to play another one. In the first critical thinking class, we always did that. But those articles that we read in the second critical thinking class were so dense and so intense, I had a hard time concentrating. It's easier for me to learn when I can tie it to something that I already know. That's just basic learning. If there's experience involved, it seems to work better for me. Theory is better when it's combined with practice, rather than just straight theory. Show me how this has worked. Who's used this? I am more drawn to things that I can take back to my job or back to the classroom.

For my current class we have to write a research proposal and a design. I think it will be real helpful in pushing me. I think that's what I need. Left to my own devices it doesn't seem to be working real well. There's too many things that I'm interested in and I can't seem to narrow it down. I can't seem to focus. In two weeks, I think I changed topics three times. I just couldn't stick with it. I was forced to go through it step by step by step and for me it's always a lot of writing and crossing out. I write it all out and I cross it out and see what I'm left with. You know, until somebody says to me, "You're headed in the right direction," or "Keep going with that," I think it's just going to be a struggle. I have to have this assignment done by Wednesday and I guess I just need that push from my chair. Left to my own devices, I just wasn't doing it. This semester in trying to choose a topic, I see what happens when I'm given too much freedom. When I need to figure it out by myself without the pressures of time, I just don't do it. What the structure of this class has forced me to do is really focus on what I want to do and what the research is going to look like. A topic I was interested in was how mothers influence their daughters in terms of education and expectations. It started with a conversation that I had with Keri when she was—well—anyway—you know how good I am with issues of time.

And as for how long I have been working on this degree I really can't answer. Maybe it's been a couple of years? Two years? Three years? I started out thinking I was just going to take one class and take my time. Of course, I could not do that. Instead, I started taking two or three—so I probably came through quicker than I had anticipated. If I had not taken as many courses at a time, I'd lose momentum, and once I lose momentum, it's really difficult for me to keep going. The more classes you take, the less you realize you know. I am using this opportunity to explore that. I don't think I will continue in formal education, but I can't see it ever stopping. I'm already thinking about what I'm going to do when this is done and I'm nowhere near being done. Maybe that's a coping strategy. I think I just get an incredible sense of accomplishment and that's really, for me, what this is about. It's not changing my job. It's not promotion. That's really what it comes down to: personal satisfaction. I started on this really hard thing and I finished it.

The adult education program has made such a difference in how I do things in the critical thinking class that I teach. I take my laptop into the family room and while I'm watching television, I go online and read what people are saying and respond. I explain to my students that I want them to be able to question what they accept. We talk about symbolic language and what that means. We talk about things like inference—taking information and using it to develop new information. I ask them, "How do you take that knowledge back to your group? And how can you make yourself a leader, if you choose to?" One of my limitations is to jump to conclusions. So we talk a lot about biases and how you know what a bias is.

Coping and Strategizing

At the time of our interviews, Marianne equated coping with the navigation of interpersonal situations and strategizing as a means to increase one's ability to learn. [Marianne's narrative concludes.]

I think a coping mechanism is just a way to make yourself comfortable with what you need to do. In a classroom setting, it would mean getting up and leaving. Even in meetings, when I feel like I just can't sit through it anymore and I know I'm not paying any attention to what's happening, I may as well get up and leave, just to move around a little bit. I guess that's what I would call a coping mechanism: to make yourself comfortable with what you need to do, and to realize what your limitations are in terms of time and attention. I guess I see coping as having to find a way to deal with things like frustration. I think learning strategies are more like the note-taking and other things that I've talked about. Coping would be more social: how you interact with other people. I have a pretty low frustration level at times and if I'm not coping with it I'm probably doing things that I'm going to regret and saying things I wish I hadn't said. I was somebody who, when I became angry, I lost my temper. Once you start doing that repeatedly you realize that's what people's perception of you is. And that wasn't how I thought of myself at all. I thought of myself as logical and rational, and finally realized that if I wanted to be perceived that way that I couldn't have these outbursts and expect people just to disregard them. I would say things like, "What were you thinking?" Instead of, "I don't understand your decision. Could you explain it to me?" Finally, I started reading facial expressions and realizing—oh, man—I'm losing my message because of the way it's being delivered. People aren't taking me seriously because of the way that I'm saying what I'm saying. If I really want to accomplish something, I'm going to have to say what I want to say in a way that's more acceptable.

A learning strategy would be directly related to school. You know, I've always enjoyed school. I think strategies help me to do that. If I didn't have strategies it'd be pretty painful, and I don't think I'd be in the doctoral program. If I hadn't figured some of that out, school wouldn't be a good thing. I guess that's because I hated that feeling of going to class and not being prepared. I hated that feeling. If I was supposed to have a *blue book,* but for some reason I was daydreaming when the announcement was made, I would start thinking of what I need to do if I didn't want that to happen again. I think it came to me as common sense. Just write everything down and review everything that the instructor gives me. If I go on my memory, I won't remember it.

There's just one other thing. It's not really a learning strategy, but it's something that I've always done. It has to do with movement: not being able to sit still and finding ways to compensate for that. I think what I've realized with me is that something's always moving. Just like your fingers are always moving, I'm always doing something like that, and that has really helped me to concentrate. Being forced to sit still and not being able to move just throws me. It completely throws me off. Yeah. I do that. I do this. I do pens. I shift positions. It's random. Crossing your leg. Kicking your foot. I don't think it's one thing in particular. Sometimes it's just doodling.

Regarding Marianne's Self-Understanding

Given her early experience of academic success combined with the fact that her classroom behavior failed to draw attention, Marianne had no reason to suspect that she was somehow different from her peers. Even though she recalled having an early awareness of numerous, specific problems related to school expectations, because of her identification as just another student, Marianne was able to accept her situation as a matter of fact. She tempered her awareness of her math weakness (for example) by an awareness of her literary strengths. Reasoning that the aptitudes of some people were simply less balanced than those of others, Marianne dismissed the discrepancy.

Upon realizing that her daughter's problematic school experiences mirrored those of her youth, Marianne sought diagnosis at the same time as her daughter. Although the literature cites a period of post-diagnosis mourning as a common experience during which time an individual comes to terms with the condition's permanence (Fisher, 1998), that this period slipped past with little fanfare was congruent with Marianne's predilection for linear problem solving: determine the problem; devise a solution; proceed toward the goal. In recognition of her compensatory ability, Marianne questioned the necessity of treating her symptoms with medication. She also made reference to her belief that having AD/HD makes a person think more creatively. In essence, Marianne's position was that having AD/HD has made it possible for her to compensate for AD/HD.

Her awareness of specific problems came from two primary sources. The first was a result of her keen sense of motivation. Given her drive to progress, whenever an obstacle presented itself Marianne quickly recognized the impediment. The second stemmed from having been diagnosed. Knowledge of the disorder allowed Marianne to revisit past experience and to reevaluate those outcomes she had been unhappy with. Desirous of a more professional persona, Marianne increased her level of self-monitoring. Applied more generally, self-understanding has allowed Marianne to seek out and conceptually dismantle obstacles before they present a problem. Even so, Marianne freely admitted that she has continued to do things that are wrong without realizing it. Illustrative of the ongoing nature of her task was the announcement of several realizations made during our interviews.

In situations where she could not find a conceptual solution to an obstacle, Marianne looked for external ways to cope. Aware that a promotion would mean more time spent in committee, for example, led Marianne to avoid the position. At times, Marianne candidly shared limitations likely to remain. Whenever one of my questions concerned dates, for example, Marianne simply reminded me (often with a lilt) that she was unlikely to provide an accurate response. Similarly, Marianne's habit of interrupting others lacked a corrective plan. Overall, Marianne's depth of self-understanding has allowed her the option of modifying her actions or her environment in ways that have served her well.

6

DIANE:
"I learned to cope in some ways very well."

At the time of our first interview, Diane was a fifty-three year old doctoral student diagnosed with AD/HD at age thirty-nine. Many of Diane's experiences centered upon proving herself an able learner. I found her sense of humor quite enjoyable, although it did not translate as well as I had hoped. At issue was Diane's frequent reliance on the use of hand gestures or expressions to convey humor, and on occasion to finish a thought. Each of our meetings took place during the midmorning hours in a classroom at her present workplace. Our first interview took place one day after my third interview with Marianne. (Throughout the duration of our first interview, Diane tapped her coffee cup on the table.)

Experiences of Youth

Diane's youthful experience of formal learning was fraught with contradiction. Paired with her remarkable reading comprehension was a difficulty understanding the spoken word. Despite considerable efforts taken outside the classroom, her in-class experience was a hodge-podge of boredom, confusion, clowning, and self-castigation. [Diane's narrative begins.]

I went right into first grade. I never did go through kindergarten. In first grade, we took a test in reading comprehension. At that time, it was first grade through eighth grade in a one-room schoolhouse. I got one hundred percent and beat out all the eighth graders in comprehension, yet I couldn't speak clearly. When I hear words, they sound scrambled. The teacher who first said that I was not speaking clearly thought it was because I was lazy, so she would keep me after school. I was probably eight or nine. Probably the first time I knew something was wrong was

51

when I was in grade school and we were all supposed to do this Maypole dance. We were supposed to skip and I couldn't skip. The teacher thought I was doing it on purpose so she sent me home. It's really embarrassing to have to learn how to skip. To stop the focus of being seen as lazy I became the class clown, which is not that common for girls. I would go into that role because it's a lot more fun to have people laugh with you than laugh at you. I was constantly getting in trouble at school because I couldn't sit still. I could comprehend things so fast I was bored most of the time. Whenever I would look at the clock, it seemed like the hands would never move. School was just a torture, except for art class. I was very good. They picked some of my stuff to travel around the country as a child. I really got into it. I would go into my room and just paint—listen to music and paint. I also liked reading, but I could do that on my own.

I started taking Latin because it was the only foreign language offered at our Catholic high school. I really couldn't understand it, having trouble with my mind floating out the window and wondering what the farmer's doing across the field. I would lose it. Those Latin classes were the longest hours in my life. They'd have you write essays on stupid things. The Latin teacher caught me talking on the first or second day and assigned me five hundred words on when to talk and when not to talk. So, I did it in a very sarcastic way. He wound up reading it to the class, who all thought it was hilarious. I found it a little embarrassing. There was another time in history class that I had to write a one thousand-word essay on the hippopotamus. In response, I drew a hippopotamus and I wrote "1000 words" above it and gave it to the instructor. That got me into trouble. I just kind of floated.

When we started mathematics, it would just drop out of my head. In high school algebra the teacher gave me a "P" for passing. They never gave a grade of "P" before or since at the school. She was a new teacher and she said, "I don't understand. She tries so hard." I would do some of the steps in my mind and could come up with the correct answer sometimes, but I couldn't do the steps we were supposed to. When grades were due, she gave me a "P." After that, I decided algebra wasn't for me. My grades were like roller coasters. Anything that had to do with math and rote logical stuff I didn't do so well at—but religion and history? I was really good at history.

I also had trouble telling my right hand from my left hand all my life, so about the time I was a sophomore or junior in high school I decided to wear a ring on my left hand, so when I looked down I would know, that's my left hand. Someone would say, "Go down this hallway and turn left," and I'd go down the hallway and turn right. If they said, "Drive to the right or left," I'd have no idea.

Part way through high school I started taking courses that weren't necessarily college-level, even though I had intended to go to college. They were what our school referred to as the dumb courses. I was labeled again. The thing is, I had two sisters that were older than me that did wonderfully and I was always being compared. One time, in the principal's office I was asked, "Why can't you be more like your sisters?" Nothing I did seemed to be good enough. Nothing I tried seemed to work out well. It seemed like when I tried harder, I would flub it up more. Around then, I really pulled back from trying to learn. High school is when it really hit me. I started thinking that if I couldn't handle those college prep classes I must be dumb. As it was, I had low interest, low self-esteem, and low involvement. The only reason I didn't kill myself is I thought if I did, I'd go to Hell. Then when I was fifteen, the brother at the seminary asked me if I would work as a secretary. And a girl moved in from another town and became my friend. These key people kind of pulled me out of myself and I managed to start living. Before then, I considered myself kind of dead, just going along with the process. I was just learning to get out of school at that time. Just graduate. That's all I wanted to do. I didn't care if I saw that school again. I just wanted to get out of there. I was still getting in a lot of trouble because I was always talking. School was not fun. Yet, there was always this great need to know. I think most of my learning took place outside of school where I could learn on my own. I did much better learning on my own than in a regimented classroom.

I took this IQ test and when it came back, all of a sudden, I was ushered into the counselor's office and they said, "You should be doing better than you're doing here." Okay. Nobody ever cared before. How come all of a sudden they're caring? My parents would push my sisters and brothers, but they'd get my report card and say, "Oh this is very good for you." That's what I would get. Then all of a sudden their attitudes changed. They asked, "Why are you giving up, doing this mediocre stuff?" Another thing that changed around this time is that I started doing coffee. I drink a lot of coffee even now, because it's just like a tranquilizer for my body. People think that's weird. If I drink enough of it I will get very sleepy. I drink it at meetings where I know that I have to be sitting still. I will continually drink it because it helps a lot. Around the same time as starting on coffee, I found out that I was milk intolerant. When I started having coffee and toast, I started feeling better. Although I hardly drank in high school, if I knew I had a test coming, I would have a small screwdriver before class. I did that six or seven times.

I learned to cope in some ways very well. Our high school history classes were big on dates so I would use flash cards. I would get up early the day of the test and study these flash cards for twenty minutes. Then I'd be fine when I took the test. I could remember, but I couldn't over-study. It just had to be about twenty minutes. I would put it on a short card, close my eyes, and visualize it like I'm taking a snapshot. It would be imprinted on my mind and I could remember. Then I would go to the next one. I would use stories to connect concepts to my experiences; or I would repeat something to myself until I could say it word for word. Other times, I could study all night. Before taking a spelling test, I could spell them to my mother perfectly. Then the test would come and I would freeze. So, I used to write my vocabulary words in pencil on the desk. Does that count as a strategy? At our home, we always used humor too. In our home—oh my goodness—if you didn't have a sense of humor you'd be dead. On my mother's side, life was to be enjoyed no matter what came up. That was a way of living at home.

Adulthood Experiences

Upon graduating from high school, Diane managed to recast herself as having the ability to succeed as a learner. Although she would continue to face challenges, as well as setbacks, her rise in confidence gave her the power to choose who she would become.

Everybody I knew, myself included, thought I was stupid and I wanted to prove to the world that I wasn't stupid. My idea was to be a teacher because I figured they did such a bad job on me that I could do better. Part of it was process of elimination. When I was growing up a woman was a nurse, a teacher, or maybe a secretary. There weren't too many things out there at first. I think it was in high school that I began looking at some of these teachers and thinking, I know I can do a better job than this. That's when I decided to become a teacher. And you had to go to college to be a teacher. I loved to read and I loved to learn, but my main focus was to get the degree so people didn't think I was stupid.

I would say I was always a self-directed learner because I would always have books from the library that I was reading. I loved going places in my mind and thinking of different possibilities. That kept me going. The people that I grew up with in Iowa sometimes were very small-minded. I went with a lot of farmers and so you'd hear about the day milking and the night milking and what new tractor they were going to buy and I found that so boring. I wanted to know what was going on in China. The girls only wanted to talk about boyfriends and I didn't have much interest in that. I liked boys but I'm not going to spend eight hours a day talking about them. I love my husband but I don't spend twenty hours a day talking about him. Going to college gave me a great opportunity to expand.

It was in college that I really noticed there was a problem with my hearing. I went to the center to get my hearing tested and the weird thing was, my hearing was fine. They tested for sounds. In fact, I can hear higher better sounds than most people can. I can hear sounds that some animals aren't supposed to hear. When it came to the low sounds, I did have some problems. Even now when I say words that I've learned how to hear and say them correctly, it sounds weird. Like the word "grandma." I hear grandma kind of as "ga-uh." That's how I hear it. I've been told you say grandma, or grandmother. I don't hear it that way. I'm only talking that way because that's how I've been told how to say it. Learning a new word is very hard and there are some words I can't say. I'll have my friends repeat a word over and over again. Sometimes I spell it out in little pieces so I can pick up how to say the word. In graduate school, there are terms like epistemology. I'll write them out and practice them. Phenomenology: it was five weeks before I could say that.

Another problem in college was that I had to take mathematics and I had to take a language. In the beginning, I was okay in math. Then it got complicated so I skipped class and earned an "F." The second time I figured if I did really well at the midterm, I could do really bad at the rest of it and it wouldn't matter, so I had my future husband—who was my boyfriend then—tutor me. I aced the midterm and showed periodically for classes. I ended up passing, but language was a problem. The first semester was okay because we just had to write things. The next semester we had to speak it. In class, we wore headphones and we were to repeat what the teacher said. I really wanted to learn Spanish and I thought I was doing a good job when the teacher came over, tapped me on the shoulder and said, "Quit fooling around." Okay. During the next class he pulled me out and said, "I want you to quit fooling around in class or I'm going to kick you out." At that time, I hadn't figured out that I scrambled sounds. I thought that I was doing the best I could. The third time he pulled me out of class. Sitting in the student union afterwards I talked with this stranger who sat down beside me and I started telling him that I didn't know how I was going to graduate. I wanted to become a teacher and I needed to have a degree to teach. He told me about this degree called the bachelor's of general studies. I switched schools and was able to get through college.

Although I did earn a teaching certification, I didn't keep it up when I moved out of state. Other than Bible study, I never did go into teaching. I didn't have enough self-confidence and every time I student taught I would wind up with a migraine headache. It was probably when I was at the Hispanic church teaching Bible study that I discovered I really liked working with the adults. People would come up to me who could speak almost no English and yet I would understand what they wanted. It's just like with the Polish lady that took care of my mother-in-law who was going through dementia. Although the lady didn't speak much English, the two of us kind of just communicated. When my mother-in-law's friend Agnes, who did speak Polish, came in I said, "Oh, this is really a shame that her son has stomach cancer." Agnes said, "No. I don't think so." Then I said, "Well, maybe I misunderstood because I really don't speak Polish, but that's what I thought she was telling me." Then Agnes began talking to her and discovered that her son did have stomach cancer. The lady was in distress and somehow I understood.

You know that's interesting. I've never thought about this before. Even before I started learning about theories, because I know what things don't work well with me, I would try to make learning easier for everyone. When I would do something, I tried to involve everyone's senses. For me, the story is very important. Involve someone in their own experience of whatever it is and they can tell their story. Part of adult learning, a very important part, is respect for the individuals. They have as much to teach me, as I have to teach them. Perhaps that's one reason adult education has fascinated me. This was something that I was already doing. It was probably because of the ways in which I could not learn that I incorporated a lot of different things into my style. I never really thought about why I was doing it that way. It's just that I knew what didn't work for me, so I wasn't going to do it.

Point of Diagnosis

One of Diane's assets as a learner has been the tenacity with which she has repeatedly confronted adversity. Her initial aversion to diagnosis led Diane to seek more information. In response to exam-induced anxiety, Diane sought classes that offered alternatives. As her number of compensatory skills and strategies grew, so too did her interest in self-discovery.

While working at a financial office, I really started noticing that there was something wrong with me because I kept transposing the numbers again. Around this time, we visited my cousin and her family in Chicago and we all went to the Museum of Science and Industry to walk through the big heart. I remember that I was listening to the thump of the big heart and just as I was coming out I heard my husband saying, "Diane! Diane! I have to show this to you! It's you! It's you!" And I'm like, "What are you talking about?" He brings me to a setup where they had a person talking about learning disabilities. She was saying she didn't know how to skip, couldn't tie her shoes. That was another one of my trials as a kid: tying my shoes. Just hearing this, I knew it was me. I thought I'm not lazy, dumb, or stupid. There's something in me that is not working correctly. They had a list of places that would test in the area, so I went to this psychiatrist, got tested, and found out that I had dyslexia and then the combined hyperactivity? I could take the dyslexia. But being labeled hyperactive—I fought with the doctor on that. He said that they were amazed that I was able to get through college. He said that there were different ways that ADD could be manifest. He asked me things like, "Do you ever blank out when you're in a meeting? Does your mind go off course?" Well of course. You know, constantly. "Do I live with clutter?" Yeah. You know—I try to clean it up and there it is again. To everything he asked, I had to say, "Yes." Yet, I didn't want that label. I don't know why. The dyslexia was okay, but this other one wasn't. Then he said, "Well, this is the one that will probably pay the bill—not the dyslexia. I want you to know that." I kind of looked at him and said, "Well I guess it's okay then." They gave me some medication, but I didn't find that helped without side effects. I didn't want to live on drugs that I didn't have to take. That's the time I think I started stepping up with the coffee.

At first, the diagnosis was just such a shock. I wasn't ready for the label. I think that was because most of the people I had seen with the ADD label were boys in school who seemed to fit the category of dumb—and I didn't want to be in that category. Then I started researching and the more I did the more I realized that the doctor's diagnosis was true.

Then, because of my dyslexia, there are words that if they have a certain letter of the alphabet, I have trouble remembering them. I have terrible trouble with anybody's name that begins with a J or an L. I had a friend for twenty years and one day I was trying to introduce her to somebody and I couldn't remember her name. The whole time I knew her, I had trouble remembering her name. Nowadays I "double-think." I'd ask myself, "Does her name begin with a J or an L?" I'd tell myself, "It must, because they're the ones that act like holes in my brain." I discovered this after reading about a kid in this book. Well, he was twenty-four at the time. Anyway, he would clay out the alphabet: literally make the alphabet so that you can see it. I'm a very visual person. When I finished it, I looked down and within my alphabet; I saw that I had missed letters. Those are the letters I now know I have trouble with. The letter B is another one because it flips on me. It's weird how the brain does these tricks. I started really looking at my life around this time. You know? Like when it comes to dates and times, there's no sense of dates and time. It was then that I started finding ways to change things.

If I had a meeting, for example, I could write down the time and then have the other person check it. Before then, I would miss a lot of meetings because it would be all twirled in my head. I couldn't deny it anymore. In fact, I think the ADD caused more problems in my life than the dyslexia. Anyway, once I got over the shock and started reading what the experts were recommending I realized that I already did much of it on my own anyway. I guess just to survive I've learned a lot of different coping skills. I tried using checklists and all that. The problem is that the checklist gets lost. Then where are you? I don't think those things are helpful.

While at my next job, I began to be more active in my church. I thought that there was a need for people to help, so while working at Menard's, I began taking classes at a Catholic college. They had a description of every class they offered and made the whole syllabus available ahead of time, so I could see what was required and I could eliminate ones with a written test. Because of my anxiety, as you probably can understand, I don't do well. I could be talking to you and be fine, but put a test in front of me and I don't know a thing. I completely blank out. As an undergraduate student I didn't know I had dyslexia, but I had learned to have somebody reread things for me. Once I knew I had the problem, I still had friends who were willing to help. If I had to take a test on the spot, I might sit there for ten minutes wondering if I spelled "the" right. At the college, they thought I could do well, but didn't know for sure because my grades were so erratic. That's when I started doing some things different.

When I first used a tape recorder in class, I asked permission from the professor and mentioned I had a learning disability. I could see it immediately on his face that he equated it with being dumb. One time he stopped right in front of everybody and asked me, as if he was asking a young child, "Are you doing okay?" I was so embarrassed. The first course I took from him, I earned a "B." His was the first course that I took at the Catholic college. I also took my last course with him. Of course, he didn't remember who I was, but I ended up being one of his best students. I had the terms down. I had the practical experience. I aced that course. I don't use a tape recorder so much anymore because of the way things are taught here. Now there's all this new technology, like cell phones, that have been a blessing. Recently, I discovered a pen that you can use to scan words right from the page and—using *Bluetooth* technology—put it into your computer. It's really great for taking notes and incorporating them into your paper, especially because when I write something with pen and paper and I look at it, I can't figure out what I wrote.

Considering Adult Education

Much of Diane's interest in adult education was rooted in having overcome her own barriers to learning and her desire to help others do likewise. A mix of spirituality, an interest in social justice, and a sense of pragmatism provided the extra push.

My interest in adult education probably started when I was at the Catholic college. Because I've had to struggle so hard to learn, I wanted to help others to learn easily as possible. When I took my first class in adult learning, I didn't even realize that there was a difference between how children learned and how adults learned. We read some articles about it and I found it extremely interesting. The material wasn't that in-depth, but Sister Jean practiced it in her classroom. To me it was like when I was a kid sitting in eighth grade saying, "There's got to be better ways to learn than this. And I know I can do better as a teacher." In Sister Jean's class, I could fully use my learning skills. There was something there that I knew could be broadcast and I wanted to learn more about it. I would say it was a breakthrough moment because it was just an eye-opening experience.

To be a woman in the Catholic Church and want others to listen to your opinion, it helps to have a doctorate behind your name. I just had this sense that I should go on for my doctorate. I felt God didn't send me here to fail. I think that's where the determination comes in for me. It's my faith. At first I wasn't sure if I wanted a doctorate of theology or a doctorate of education so I was really testing this school when I decided to take the first course in adult education and started reading books on adult education. A lot of the books said that this school had the best adult education program in the nation. I found myself very excited, not just by what we were learning, but by way the class was taught. The professor was using the learning theories in class and I was learning so much so quickly. I also was impressed by the students and all the different reasons they had for going into it. They were concerned about the society and social justice and about people in general. In that first class I thought, these people are trying to make the world better. Most of them are so accepting of you that, especially within a small group, everyone wants to do their best. You actually do better than you even know you can and I think that starts building your self-esteem. Between my spiritual director and me, we thought enrolling in the adult education program was the right decision.

The Graduate School Experience

Reminiscent of the section detailing Diane's first experiences with formal learning, the following narrative contains a mixture of emotions, discoveries, excitements, setbacks, and periods of growth. Unlike her youth, where Diane learned to reject herself, her cumulative experience of being a doctoral student was, to date, stridently unapologetic and forward thinking.

As I've taken courses, each of the professors have shown that they're concerned about each one of us. They're not just concerned with us learning how to learn or teaching others how to learn. They're concerned about us as individuals. They're concerned about the world. They're trying to do their best to make the world a better place. I've probably overstated this point, but it seems like there's so much more than just trying to learn what is written. Normally in the classroom environment, teachers are still just talking to you. I have a terrible time with people just talking. In adult education, there are all sorts of different ways that you get involved. I felt like I got an excellent education from the Catholic college and as I felt privileged to get into this program, I decided that I was going to make it work no matter what, even with the frustrations of being ADD.

With adult education, you can incorporate whatever works best for you. That's being self-directed. If you're enthused about it, you learn even more. I don't know if I would have made it had I went into something else. I think it's a wonderful program for someone who has Attention Deficit Disorder. Most of the time, you are free to experiment with your learning style and because a lot of it is self-directed, I think you excel even more. You push yourself even harder. Although I do resent the idea of the comprehensive final as it is. I don't believe it belongs in adult education. If they're going to have it, there ought to be different varieties for our different learning styles.

My critical thinking class is where I began to accept that this is how I am and there are ways that I am strong and other people aren't. One of the ways that I'm strong is I can grasp theories far quicker than a lot of other people. It was a very helpful class. Seeing how other people learned differently was a tremendous help in my work as an educator. I realized one of the reasons I didn't excel in grade school is that it was geared towards one kind of a learner, which I wasn't. I took the Myers-Briggs test and discovered that I have a very high intuitive sense. They say if you are high in one area you should try to balance it. So, I thought of that as not being too good. After the critical thinking class I went to Paris with several people who could speak French—something I don't do. They stopped and asked somebody in beautiful, fluent French where to go. We were looking for this author's home. He wrote *Les Miserables*. Hugo. Victor Hugo. Afterwards one said, "Well, we didn't grasp all that." And I asked, "Can I tell you what I thought?" I said, "We go down here two blocks. We turn left. We go up a hill and then it's at the top of the hill." They both kind of looked at me like: "But you don't know French." And I said, "Let's try it." So, we went the way I said and it was right there. I think it's because of my hearing. Because I don't hear a lot of things, listening is like a puzzle that I figure out. It's like I read people. As he was talking, he was using his arms and I understood from his sign language what to do. Even though I may be off-the-wall according to that Myers-Briggs test, for me it's necessary to be extreme. At first, I was a little embarrassed. Then I realized this is how I learn. I went from being ashamed of who I was as a learner to accepting that this was how God made me.

I really liked the course that I took in research. I thought it was concrete and practical. I had no knowledge of methodologies at that time so the professor recommended some books to me. My understanding of phenomenology is to interpret an event or a circumstance. Interpret is the big word, because we can't look at any experience without bringing our own life experience into it. Interpretation is a very personal act no matter what we're looking at. We're seeing it through our own lens and we all are coming from multiple intelligences. More than one person can see a thing happening. I think that phenomenology tries to get closest to the truth it possibly can. You're going to have a bias, but part of phenomenology is admitting that you have that bias. I don't think it is a pitfall as you're going to have some insight, where somebody who doesn't have the learning disability wouldn't. Admit you have a bias in this and examine that from all angles. The other advantage you have is having a committee. You have these other eyes for what you don't see and they're going to help you complete your vision.

I am in a situation right now where I have some things that need to get done, but I've been avoiding it. I've got to get it done. I can't sit there and embarrass myself. I start research by reading some books. Then the ideas are in my head as I'm doing other things and I go: ah-ha, and I start connecting things. Still, I have to have that "ah-ha" moment where I start making connections before I can sit down to write. And I kind of write papers backwards. I see the end result but I don't see the steps up to it because the concept of end result is a lot easier than all the individual concepts going on. I can't work with an outline either. I have tried and if anything, it prevents me. I can write the ending and I can write the beginning and then I can connect the dots, but I cannot sit there, write an outline, and have it make sense. Actually, before I can sit down I usually have the whole thing written in my head. I think for most people to sit there, read stuff, and try to work it out completely in your head before sitting down to write would be ridiculous. I know that's the way it goes through my mind. Just like, I was telling you how I would put things on flash cards and I would sit and remember them. That's kind of how it starts in my mind. I'll have some prayer going on. I also really believe in the power of dreams. Just sleep on it. Wake up and there it is. Other times I need adrenalin for the ideas to come. Bam! Rush! Get it done! I don't like all the anxiety with it, but when I give myself lots of time, I just sit there. You know? I have to get papers done early so that I can give them to somebody to proofread. Why do you think my house is so clean? I've been cleaning, cleaning and thinking, cleaning and thinking, cleaning and thinking.

Determination is just part of my character. If there's something I need to do, I will persist at it if it kills me. That means I may get a migraine. I may not have sleep. I may stay up all night. If that is what I have to do to get the assignment done, I do it. Then there's my husband, Newt—not his real name—who is so supportive. I probably couldn't make it through this program without him. I mean he puts gas in my car so I don't run out on the way to class. He volunteers occasionally if I need help with my papers. He even bought me a GPS so I don't get lost so much. I also have friends. And even though they may tease me about being a perpetual student, they have been very supportive. Others are praying for me. So in the long run, I know that it'll work out. I just have to get it over with.

Sometimes I look at the hyperactivity as being a gift. I can get a lot of things accomplished quicker, once I get it in my mind. It might take me a little longer up front, but once I have it, I run with it and I can accomplish a lot. Knowing that I've been against the wall before helps. I thought that my learning processes would have hindered me, but I've learned from my strategies. It worked for me, and is working for me. I think I wouldn't have discovered that if I hadn't joined this program. For example, I have learned that I can't just be sitting to learn. I can't sit in a library, just read, read, read, and learn. I can do it for short periods. Then I have to do something else. I have a very clean house when I'm trying to learn or write something. In school, they didn't give you that freedom. You had to sit in that desk. You couldn't talk to other people.

There's another thing that I've learned in college. When I go into small groups to discuss things, it stays with me so much better. In fact, that's one reason why I flunked the math class that followed African American history. After the history class, we all went to the bar. The professor went along with us. We talked about what we talked about in class. That class was one of the best ones I've ever had because of the discussions afterward. I do so much better when I work in a group.

I know when you say group work some people just groan. But I like group work. I work so much better.

Coping and Strategizing

Compared to Marianne, Diane was less able to describe her comparative conceptualization of coping skills versus learning strategies. Upon reflection, this did not surprise me. Neither was the wellspring of personal examples she provided, a surprise. [Diane's narrative concludes.]

Coping is when I bump into something—I just cope with the fact. Maybe I'll put something soft there that will help me cope with it. A learning strategy helps you almost jump over it completely. Coping is for when I knock my books on the floor. I'll just pick them up. I'll cope with this. Coping could be a matter of walking up and down the hallway a couple times or stopping what I'm doing to do something physical. Then there's a little thing I worked on my own. This sounds weird, but if I really want to concentrate on reading, I get on my exercise bike. Really, the best time for me to understand or comprehend something is while I'm exercising. I can focus so much better. I have no clue why that is. About four years ago, kind of through accident as well as sheer boredom, I was trying to read while exercising and I thought, oh. I understand this. Now that's what I do when I'm having trouble understanding something. I'll get on my exercise bike and read it. Reading while I exercise on the bike. That was a big one for me, because there are some times when I am so unfocused. I have to read something and write a report on it and I can't wrap my mind around it. Get on the exercise bike. If I'm exercising, I can concentrate.

Recently I started having a separate place for materials, if I'm taking more than one course. And the materials are color-coded. If I was taking two courses one might be green and one might be blue. I also keep material from class in one area so it's not all over the house, or in the car, or at work, or in a book. I don't have to go a thousand places. I keep all the notes together. I keep all the homework together. If possible, your desk should be uncluttered. That suggestion was meant for children, but it definitely helped me. I know that if I have a lot of stuff on my desk I'll be fiddling with it. Another skill I learned of was to use sticky-notes to post reminders, and when I get my syllabus, I make about five copies immediately. I used to get so frustrated trying to find things. You have it everywhere and then company comes. You clean up and after the company leaves and then, where are my books? What did I do with them?

Sometimes it helps to go into the ADD chat rooms and just seeing how people are frustrated. You know, the relief that I'm in welcome company? Their clutter seems worse than my clutter? Or my disorganization doesn't seem quite as bad? How they start one thing and then start another thing? Most people would look at that and think it's a terrible way to cope. Then sometimes I feel fearful and I don't know why. There's no reason. Where are these things coming from? Other times, when I have anxiety that I can't place a finger on, I do something that I can get totally involved in—like concentrate on a computer game for a while. I relax. Have some fun. That's another thing I need to talk about: fun. Humor is a wonderful asset to learning. I've found that if I go and crack a joke with a couple friends I calm down and I can work again. I took a class on using humor in adult education.

It wasn't until I was in that class that I realized how humor has been important to me throughout my life and how it will be an important ingredient to get me through all these years ahead of me. We started talking about humor and what it meant in our lives and I realized it meant a lot. Then while talking to you the other day I realized that I was using humor as a learning strategy. I've been using humor as a strategy to learn and didn't really realize it until now. I go out and talk. Laugh. Laugh. Laugh. When I come back, I'm able to concentrate. It's not even a coping mechanism. It's something that helps me to relax. It helps when the blanks come. Later you go do something and you remember the joke. Then you're double learning it.

I think these interviews have been helpful to me. Some of your questions brought a different perspective than I normally would have taken myself. I started looking at some of the things I was doing that I never would have paid attention to before. I think if anything has changed in my life, it's that I can learn as good, or better than most individuals out there, which I probably would not have said previously. It's ironic because when I went to my high school reunion while working on my master's my classmates said, "Oh yeah. We can understand that. You were always one of the smarter ones." I said, "Well I wish you would have told me. I would have felt a lot better about myself at the time."

Regarding Diane's Self-Understanding

Diane's depth of self-understanding has been mixed for many years. Her sense of being different was made both through third-person comparisons to others and through her own observations. Like Marianne, Diane exuded tenacity for problem solving and of the four informants was able to share the widest range of specific coping mechanisms. She also shared realizations made during her interviews.

Unlike Marianne, who had the tendency to problem-solve and move on, Diane was much more likely to keep a mental record of the ways in which she was different. Consequently, Diane willfully resorted to becoming a class clown as a way to draw attention away from her perceived deficiencies. Although lacking natural ability in mathematics and foreign language, Diane was well aware of her strengths in fine art and reading comprehension (having received validation for both). Like Marianne, being cognizant of her strengths has helped Diane to be less critical of her weaknesses.

Having earned a "P" for passing high school algebra (a result of effort more than mastery), Diane was steered towards the vocational curriculum. Given the contextual association that the vocational education courses were for the unintelligent, Diane assumed the unintelligent label. Confronted with low expectations and poor self-esteem, a teenaged Diane harbored self-destructive thoughts. Crediting the emergence of a small, but influential support structure at age fifteen, Diane began to find the way out. Thanks in part to this network and her high score on a high school intelligence test Diane eventually became convinced that she must be intelligent after all. With this conviction came a need to convince others of the same, thus helping to set the stage for her college education.

The long list of coping mechanisms (having worn a ring on her left hand, having used alcohol, coffee, sticky notes, *et cetera*) at her disposal is a testament to one level of self-knowledge. Despite their apparent value, the development of these mechanisms has been reactionary. As she matured, Diane began to utilize proactive methods of coping. Although she did not know about her dyslexia, Diane was quite aware that her papers were in need of a proofreader. Her consequent reliance on friends proved to be an effective way to cope. The point of transition (from reactive to increasingly proactive) for Diane was her dual diagnosis: dyslexia and AD/HD. Ironically, even as the AD/HD diagnosis allowed Diane to understand the causes behind the appearance of lacking intelligence, her mental association with "dumb boys" was concurrently reinforced.

Diane's journey in terms of both self-understanding and self-acceptance as a person and as a learner has been gradual, and at times haphazard. Helping to illuminate the ongoing nature of this process was the statement Diane made near the end of her final interview, in which she credited her participation in this study for providing a different perspective.

7

HOWARD:
"How could I be good and bad at the same time?"

At the time of our first interview, Howard was a sixty-year old master's student diagnosed with AD/HD at age forty-nine. A strong theme throughout Howard's interviews was his overwhelming sense of being perceived as a failure by those close to him. He also had a low-key sense of humor, an easy manner, and a propensity for drifting off-topic.

Experiences of Youth

With frequent moves, invalidating parents, excessive criticism at school, and stunts gone awry, the symptoms of AD/HD just added to the other difficulties Howard faced in childhood. Perhaps most damaging, was the extent to which he internalized the negativity surrounding him. [Howard's narrative begins.]

When I was in second or third grade I earned "As" and "Bs". Then as time progressed, they began to drop off. By junior high school my grades tended to be "Cs" and below. Then I failed ninth grade and almost didn't make it through my senior year in high school. At the time, ADD existed, but nobody knew it. They didn't assign it a name. My mother would have said that ADD sounds like another dumb excuse. I was labeled by my parents and by my teachers as being willfully lazy. They said if I would just get my act together, things would be a whole lot better. Instead, I reacted to that with a lot of anger.

My father is a retired Protestant minister, so we moved a lot when I was young. It gave me a sense of disconnectedness to my environment. So there were more things than just ADD that complicated my life. When I was six, eight, nine years old, I didn't really think about it. We were moving to a new place. My parents always built up the idea that it was a great thing to have happen. There are big blotches of my youth that I don't remember. I think because there was so much moving around, one thing blurred into another. If you talk to me about third and fourth grades, or fifth grade, I don't remember much of anything at all. I don't remember where I was.

I think it was around fifth grade when a teacher said I could write a paper on anything I wanted and suggested the encyclopedia as a source, that I took an early interest in Native Americans. It was just a fluke. I'd seen some old westerns on television and I'd seen westerns in the movies and how Indians were depicted and it caught on. I didn't become an expert by any stretch of the imagination, but I became very interested in it. Later on, in high school and after high school I read some material about how they were treated and distinguished between what I saw in the movies and some of the books and materials I had read. I'd go to the library and get books. I think they probably became sort of an escape, even though I wasn't a fast reader. I would get interested in a topic and then I would read. Saturday afternoons I was in reading when my friends were outside playing. Particularly in school, I'd get interested in a topic and I would hang with it. Reading wasn't a problem, but I was not an avid reader. You know, where I'd lock myself up in my room to consume a lot of information.

Eventually I became interested in World War II and in study hall when I should have been doing other things, I was reading a book. Later on, I took a much more progressive view towards things that were interesting to me back then—like how Native Americans were treated and issues related to World War II and the Vietnam War. I certainly had a contrast in my life by launching into things that I didn't know anything about and finding out about them.

As for my grades, there were comments like, "I don't know why he is this way. He certainly seems to be intelligent. Why is it that he's not cutting the grades?" Then there were threats from my parents. I played basketball in sixth grade, but after they realized how my grades were dropping off, they just took away all sports. Those were some of the earliest experiences with something being wrong and I was blaming myself for being such a disgusting disappointment to my parents. How could I have done that? Much of my school experience was spent trying to get away from the criticism about my grades and the lectures from my dad.

None of the classes in junior high were student-centered. The guy would sit there, lecture for a while, and ask questions to see if you were reading the textbook. Usually, when the teacher came around to me and asked a question, I didn't know the answer. It wasn't uncommon for a teacher to say, "Stop daydreaming." And I was. I was looking out the window, paying attention to other things. That might have been a defensive tactic because if I was looking out the window I couldn't be paying attention in class, and wouldn't be called on as much. I also picked the classes that were the easiest. In the classes that were more difficult, like math class, I justified low grades as the result of teachers not knowing how incapable I was. When they told me that I wasn't doing well, I told myself the same thing. I internalized all of that and became the focus of my own problem. I think that before high school I was navel-focused. I was focused on how I was doing, how I was adjusting, things that were affecting me. I think that there were needs that weren't being met, like the need for praise once in a while. A question that I could never answer in those earlier years was how could I be bad and good at the same time? There were other things to complicate my situation too. My father's father used to get terribly angry and would use a belt to beat his kids. All of the kids on his side of the family were affected and he carried some of it into his own family.

One time in junior high, after Christmas, I put an ad in the paper that said: "Wanted: Old Christmas Trees." I gave the address of my music teacher, but no phone number. I felt energized. Then two or three weeks went by and nothing had been said. I was biting at the bit to find out what the reaction was, so I told on myself. He said that he got several. There was one old man that showed up with a tree, hoping to get the money he spent for it. A classmate said, "Oh you know, he got two or three trees in his front yard." He made it sound as if the teacher made up part of it to make me feel worse. I still don't know what the story was. I spent the rest of the year focusing on what an idiot I was.

When I was a kid I did a lot of bike riding around town: once in a while with friends, but usually I was by myself. In ninth grade, an English teacher wanted me to turn in a book report. I wrote the report on a book that I manufactured in my head. It didn't work. She caught me red-handed. I don't know that the book report was all that well written to begin with, but for me to manufacture characters and an entire book—I think she was impressed with my effort and creativity. This went beyond all that to her. It went beyond even copying somebody else's work. Still, there wasn't any plagiarism. There wasn't any book. That was the only time.

I struggled all the way through high school. My self-esteem was absolutely in the toilet, and I was convinced that I was a disappointment to everybody. I found it difficult to make friends, but figured it wouldn't matter because I was going to move anyway. Yet, there were times in class that I could be comical, and I pulled stunts. You know? I tried to draw attention to myself to cover up what I felt were my deficiencies. Sometimes in high school, I'd come up with one-liners. The most memorable one was in response to a social studies teacher who was talking about women in history. The word feminism hadn't really been coined yet and he wanted us to discuss how the women of the day were different from women seventy-five years earlier. That's when I popped in with the one-liner, "They're older." He stopped and he thought about it. I thought I was going to get chewed out. Then he burst out with a smile and started laughing. That's when I began to find out that one-liners, well placed, could work. It was a way of drawing attention to myself. If I'm bad at my studies, I could be good at something else.

Then there was the clock. I couldn't wait to get out of class all through high school. When you don't think you're doing very well and people are critical of you, it's like a dog avoiding a shock or something. That's how I felt. When I graduated, I was absolutely, incredibly ecstatic. And because I got to graduate from a brand-new high school, none of my classmates knew that I flunked ninth grade.

Adulthood Experiences

Much of Howard's problems in adulthood were the result of his grand-scale inability to focus. Simply put, Howard often had no idea of what to do with himself. Because of having learned to self-invalidate as a child, Howard was often distrustful of his own inclinations.

After high school, my mother suggested that I go to school at the nearest state university because they would take anybody if you went in the summer. All you had to do was go prove yourself—so in the summer of 1963, I started college. Often, I did what other people wanted me to. That was how I got along in the family. Part way in, I began to realize how disinterested I was and I came up with all kinds of excuses about why, like how boring the classes were.

I knew that my notes were incredibly bad, but I didn't want to appear dumb, so I'd sit in class and I'd write some words or I'd write some brief notes on a piece of paper. I never doodled because I didn't think I could draw. Everybody around me was just scribbling away like crazy. A couple of teachers were interested in the notes of their students, but when they saw mine I think they were disappointed. There were no lessons on taking notes. The assumption was that by the time you got through high school you knew how. If they were teaching about that, I never heard it, or I wasn't listening or something. It wasn't just writing notes; it was making sure that nobody saw them. I would pretend as if I was leaning on my arm when I was really using my arm and hand to cover what I was writing. Sometimes students sitting next to me wouldn't hear something and look over to see what I've written. But they weren't going to get any set of complete notes from me. I got into the habit of doing it all the time and was pretty private about it.

I just wasn't ready for school. I started picking up odd jobs around town that teenagers could do. Finally, I joined the Navy. A week later, I got a postcard telling me to report to the Army. Turns out—if I hadn't enlisted, I would have been drafted. I thought it was a good way to get away from home. I got out from under, but for a long time their voices were still in my head. So I lived the life I thought that my parents wanted me to live. Because of the abuse, the moving around, the ADD, I just think I found a lot of ways to compensate for all the things that happened. A lot of it had to do with escape.

In boot camp, you take your choice of schools to go to. I chose to become a hospital corpsman and I sat through those classes and experienced the same things that had gone on in high school. I flunked the medical test the first time and was told to go back and re-study. I studied like crazy. I went back and took the test and I did better, but I still flunked it. I went to Guam anyway where I began to pick up things that I wasn't learning from the book, like on-the-job training. I could retain enough things by watching it happen and then doing it. My mother wasn't happy that I wasn't writing so I started sending tapes. Later, I discovered that she kept a lot of those old messages. I threw those out. They were depressing. I was complaining about how unhappy I was, wherever I was.

During my Navy days, I began to come out of my shell and communicate better with other people. Until then people generally saw me as detached. Some interpreted it as arrogance. I think my head was just somewhere else. One day a couple of corpsmen said, "Let's go out. Come on out with us, Howard." At first, I was ready to say no. I'd go stand in the chow line on the ship and I'd take a book with me on history or philosophy or something and I'd stand in line. It was a long line and I had time to read. I always had a book in my back pocket. It was my way of escaping. But I went, and we had a good time.

I was happy not to go to Vietnam. My fear was that I had not learned enough in corps school and would not be proficient enough in the field; that I would be left with a person who was bleeding to death and I wouldn't know what to do. I was going to be in a lot of hot water if I let anybody die. There was always that threat, but about a week or so before I was supposed to leave, they cancelled the orders. I finished my tour of duty, getting out early out to go back to school, which is what I wanted to do. I felt like that's where I should be.

I wanted to go back and see if I could do better. And I did. I think part of it was that I had matured. Also, I knew I wasn't going anywhere if I didn't have a college education. Some classes I did well in. In some classes, I was mediocre. Yet,

I did begin to get a better sense of self-esteem. I still had the problem with taking notes and went to this geology professor and said, "I've got this problem in class." He said, "I know," and showed me my grades. He was going to assign me a "C" or a "D." Instead, I pulled an all-nighter, went to class with my eyes half shut, sat down, took the test, and damn near aced it. I rote-memorized it enough to get by on the test and then I completely forgot it. I was so pleased with myself for having accomplished something, I told my parents.

Probably six months after I got out of the Navy I was making plans to get married. I met Kathleen in Atlanta where they had weekend conferences for youth who wanted to experience how theology related to urban life. I became attracted to that pattern of thinking. Some of the readings my dad made on Sunday mornings came from The New Testament and made a lot of sense to me. He recognized poverty. He talked about hate groups. I think over time my worldview began to change. The New Testament began to sensitize me to other people. When I became involved with the peace movement locally, I noticed that Kathleen didn't like it. I was much more liberal than she was.

After earning my bachelor's degree in general studies, I couldn't decide what I wanted to do. I thought I wanted to become a minister. It was a disaster. I dropped out. Eventually we moved away and I just muddled after that. I got out of one company and went into another one. After a year of working at Kentucky Fried Chicken, I went over to Taco Bell—so stupid—as a manager trainee. I got tired of that when a little girl told me I was cutting the tomatoes the wrong way and might cut my finger. There was a period where I changed jobs three or four times in one year. I just couldn't seem to latch on to anything that I really wanted to do. Teaching was the furthest thing from my mind. One day I thought about the geology exam that I nearly aced. I went home, looked in the phone book, earmarked a page that listed geology and testing and was hired by a company that did soil testing at construction sites. I stayed with that company for thirteen years. I began to talk to people and make a few superficial friends, but I felt I could do better. I remembered my parents telling me, "You have a brain. You're not using it." I had been working this job for two years when my first wife divorced me. She thought that I could do a whole lot better than what I was doing. I know ADD people have problems with marriages. I certainly could say I've had my share of problems. I'm on my third marriage.

Point of Diagnosis

Although procrastination held up his diagnosis for a time, once it was established that he had AD/HD, the decision concerning what to do about it was prompt. In addition to medications, Howard took other actions in the attempt to improve his situation and stated quite plainly that he was experiencing an upturn even before starting treatment.

I was off and on depressed about my first marriage dissolving and I ended up beating on myself about the divorce. I also began to reflect on the fact that my oldest son had been diagnosed with ADD in junior high school and that I probably had it and should go get looked at—but I procrastinated. At the time he was diagnosed, adults didn't have ADD. We outgrew it. My ex-wife encouraged me. Then my father started encouraging me to go. One day I just stepped into an office, started the process, and came to find out that's what I had. Once I was told, I was put on Ritalin pretty much right away, but if you're trying to make a connection between taking Ritalin and having a sense of doing well, I don't think that connection was there. I was getting the sense that I was doing better before I was diagnosed. [In my attempt to establish a firm sequence of events, I inquired about his use of Ritalin. From his response, I suspect that Howard may have misconstrued my inquiry for opinion.]

Usually, I take the Ritalin first thing in the morning and if I'm going to teach a class later, I'll probably take one or two. If I take it late in the day, I wind up staying awake too long in the evening. I don't think much about myself as a learner when I'm doing it. I just know that I take it a day or a week at a time. Then I'll look back and reflect on it. I'll find techniques for getting through class. One of them is to make sure I've taken my Ritalin before I go in. And if I forget, I'll take something with caffeine in it. It's always a stimulant that keeps me aware of what's going on. Sometimes it has nothing to do with ADD. Sometimes it's a matter of having gotten four hours of sleep the night before. I don't know how Ritalin has helped me to learn or to keep learning. I was told that Ritalin is not a cure-all. It opens the door and allows you to think in a new way and to get rid of some of your old habits. Some people think you just take this medication and everything will be all right. It doesn't work that way. One thing that I have a problem with is distractions. It doesn't happen in classrooms because things are quiet—unless somebody near me is whispering—but if I am in a restaurant, I just go nuts. I'll almost shut down. Because there are so many multiple distractions going on, I tend to ignore everything. And Ritalin doesn't get rid of this stuff. It just stays and goes on and on and on.

I was in a men's group for a while. I went for about three months and then I just cut out. I just couldn't identify with it. I'm probably one of those typical men whose culture says, men don't go out, spilling their guts and crying on each other's shoulders. You know, you stay around the yard and talk about tractors and car parts. You sort of bury those things. Then you get into groups with certain friends and you feel like you can let your hair down a little bit more, but not too much. You do things that people really don't understand and you want people to understand, but it's a pain in the butt to go around explaining to everybody. You know, you can't explain to a police officer after he's pulled you over for speeding that you've got ADD, because he doesn't give a hoot. And when there is something that you would like to go back and correct, maybe you can and maybe you can't. Then if you do, it makes it look like you're putting an emphasis on it and calling attention to it. When I open up like that, I usually find that people are much more understanding than I thought they were. And I don't understand because I come from critical parents. I can get critical of other people and critical of myself at the same time. These things all, sort of, blend together. I don't know how much of it is related to ADD and how much to assign to other problems early in my life. I think it's also an interpretation of what I think is happening.

Self-help books are popular, but unless they directly address a specific issue in my life, I tend to avoid them. There's a lot of emphasis on feeling—feeling this—feeling that. Isn't that how self-help books are designed? There's nothing wrong with feelings, but to dwell on them is to make it sound like your feelings are at the center of the universe just because they're yours. For me the initial grieving was all over about how much time was wasted. Even now, I feel like ADD was the primary, or maybe the only, thing that really stood in my way. Perhaps if I had known about it sooner, or didn't have it, I think I probably would have earned degrees faster. I understand that there are people my age in school, but most of them don't have ADD. One thing that is not going to go away is feeling as if I'm making a fool out of myself and then thinking that if people only understood more about ADD, I might be able to say, "Oh. I had an ADD moment," which is what some people do. But you can't just shove a copy of an ADD book under everybody's face, ask him or her to read it, and hope that they'll understand you. Something that Ritalin doesn't undo very easily are my issues with self-esteem. They just keep popping up all the time.

Considering Adult Education

Although a long time passed between first envisioning himself as an educator and entering a graduate program in adult education, once the idea of becoming a teacher took hold, he remained committed to it. Such perseverance was in stark contrast to so many of his earlier experiences.

I got to the point where I didn't want to do construction site work any more and I really wanted to go back to school. I thought about becoming a high school English teacher. I don't know why. It just began to grow on me like a mushroom and I began to imagine myself in a classroom with students who were paying attention, reading books, and writing paragraphs. It had some sort of appeal. I had a few letters to the editor appear in newspapers and I was told that a few of my past school papers were not bad. I thought that perhaps I could develop in that area. I had taken a personality test years ago that showed that I would be good in such situations as social work. Then after my second divorce, I started taking night classes.

A friend of mine asked, "Oh, you're looking for work? You don't like your company anymore? You want to teach part-time? I know where they're looking for teachers." On his suggestion, I went over and I was hired teaching English to adult immigrants. I decided to get into teaching adult immigrants full time. It was like being a substitute teacher. They said, "If you have a degree, here's a book. Go teach." Some of the ESL programs weren't well defined. I wanted to get back to school and my current wife began asking, "Why don't you just go back and get everything done and go look for a job in adult education?" At the same time, I started to realize that there are not very many full-time jobs available for an ESL teacher. Those jobs are few and far between and there are people more qualified than me. I waited until winter to quit the construction site job because winter wasn't their busy season.

The Graduate School Experience

Howard clearly expressed a sense of value in his present program—it has helped him to focus. He has become better able to acknowledge his strengths (although not consistently). Perhaps most promising to his immediate future is the extent to which he has recently been able to accept himself as he is.

I came into the program quite by accident, looking for something like teaching high school. Then when I realized that I could enroll in a master's of adult education with a bachelor's of general studies I felt like I was making up for lost time. I was also a lot more focused, although I started having these lapses where I would get depressed over a class and feel like I was falling backwards. I'd ask myself, "What do I need to do? Take more Ritalin?"

This degree is not unlike my general arts degree. Starting with a loose knit, yet organized core, you can take it any direction that you want to. Adult education can also be loaded with teachers and students who are liberally minded. Because social movements have appealed to me for decades, I took a class on the history of unions that was taught by a socialist instructor. I also took a required qualitative research class. My project involved sitting in a conspicuous place and taking note of the body language of people passing me. Some said, "Hello," or "How are you?" Sometimes I was ignored. Other times I was treated with some sort of suspicion. All this was played out in body language. It was something that I drummed up on my own and ran with. Another project was to interview substitute teachers. A few of the instructors were boring. Others were interesting. It wasn't any different from high school. Now that I'm older, I'm on good terms with classmates. I opened up and communicated and they communicated with me. Then sometimes I would just as soon blend in. When I work with a group I can be afraid that they'll discover how little there is that I can contribute. When you've got no clue as to what you're talking about, your brain can get rattled.

Self-direction and student-centered classrooms have been a positive force for me. I like student-centered classrooms up to a point. Part of the problem is some of the college professors treat the classroom the same way high school teachers do these days, that you automatically become student-centered whenever you use small groups. I know there's some criticism about small groups that you can overwork them. I subbed in a classroom once where the teacher wanted the students to form small groups. After I read the directions for the class, one student said, "Oh. I suppose we're going to work in small groups again. I'm getting really tired of that." I happen to enjoy small groups and alternative ways of teaching. One thing I enjoy is assisting groups to move along, and if something doesn't work, I'll just drop it and do something else. It feeds my notion of what teaching can be. I've had a lot of that in adult education. Another thing I like is that they test in a way that is comfortable for me. To this day, the classes that I enjoy the most are the ones where you're required to write papers. Sitting there with a *blue book*, even now, scares the shit out of me.

Then I've always had the sense that I was never good enough in the area I was about to graduate. Sometimes when I've gotten an "A," I felt like I didn't deserve it. I think it's part of the old self-esteem problem that I'm probably going to have with me for the rest of my life. I still have this sense of failure. I've had three wives come to pretty much the same conclusion and have not been reluctant in pointing it out. They all said something that my father used to say, and my teachers used to say decades ago. "There's a problem here. You've got a problem."

Here I am—five years away from somebody's idea of retirement age—and I'm just graduating with my master's in adult education. I know that there are people in school who are my age. I know that. I also know that they are getting their doctorates. I feel that I've cheated myself out of time by not knowing what was going on, and I have this sense of guilt from not providing my fair share of family support. You know, a lot of things from the past that don't hit you right away will catch up to you later. Now there's a full-time job opening at the university that I might qualify for. The scary part for me is that I would end up sitting behind a computer for four or five hours a day, organizing stuff, which is exactly what I don't want.

I've got a class that I need to finish up now. Actually, I took the class and I didn't make it through. I had one paper due and I couldn't get the paper done. I had some sort of a writer's block or something. I was told that I could take it into the next semester. I had a deadline, and on the last day, I turned in half a paper and the half I turned in wasn't very good. Because I could not get the paper finished by the end of the following semester, I had to take the whole class over again. Now that's embarrassing as hell. I feel like I'm going backwards. The guy in charge of the student accessibility program interviewed me and the only thing he could do to help me was give me a time extension if a test came up or I could take the test there. In my case it didn't work. With class papers, giving me an extra ten minutes isn't going to help.

I'm also in a family situation now that pulls out some of those old negative feelings about myself that I used to have a long time ago, and thought I had gotten away from. It affects me profoundly now. I don't understand my current wife and don't know what to do for her in the same way that others didn't know how to handle me. It's kind of a peculiar situation and I probably hadn't thought about it until just now. Then I'll have some periods of mild depression that I don't know what to do with. It may last a couple of days. It may last a couple of weeks. And then I'll get these little highlights in the middle of my day that really make getting out of bed worthwhile. At other times, it's one gaffe after another. I should have just gone on back to bed and stayed there. I know what my problems are. I don't know that I look at myself as really intelligent or really dumb, though. I don't think of myself in those terms. I just think of myself as: this is who I am. This is what I would like to do.

I don't beat myself up as much lately. I say, "Wow. I got that done in the nick of time." On the other hand, I do look backward and ask myself, "What went wrong?" I still get things done at the last minute. Then I think: I'll do better next time. It's almost like wanting to go back and satisfy those childhood needs that never really got satisfied. For all those teachers who said, "You're so full of shit. You are better than you think you are and you're not doing the work," I just want to go back and answer those old voices. Part of the survival thing over this is being able to look ahead and pat myself on the shoulder. Then I feel guilty when people say, "You're really not the person I thought you were." And half of me says, "Well, you know, you're really right. I'm this pathetic little creature who really ought to be kicked." And there's another side of me that didn't used to exist that says, "Well, screw you." You know? To say screw you—for me to say that—I think it's healthy.

Coping and Strategizing

Unlike the previous informants (both of whom were enrolled in doctoral programs), Howard did not expound on his understanding of the conceptual differences between coping and strategizing. Interestingly, although Howard shared some knowledge of compensatory options, and despite being the only informant taking prescription medication to temper the symptoms of AD/HD, he admitted a failure to implement most of the options available to him. [Howard's narrative concludes.]

I've also been teaching in a program set up to encourage low-income youth to come and apply here. It's giving students a second chance by teaching them about study skills. There are some students I suspect have ADD and they aren't ever going to get any help because they haven't been diagnosed with it. We're trying to turn them around and teach them new ways of thinking and helping them to become immersed in the material so that they can find out how to ask the questions that need to be asked. I showed the movie *Bowling for Columbine* as an example of critical thinking. Here's a guy who makes up his own questions. He asks the questions that most other people might not want to ask. Yet, here I am teaching my students to do things that I don't do myself. Plan your day. I don't do that. I'm preaching what I don't practice. It's as if I'm talking to myself as much as I am to them. I know that, but then I'll go an entire semester without a daily schedule. Anything that I teach them to do, I don't do. When a paper is due, I'll pull an all-nighter just to get it done. If I have a schedule, I can stick to it fairly closely. If I'm not given some sort of organization for my day, I'll shoot time. I'll wander from one thing to another because I didn't write a schedule for myself, and when I don't have the sense of urgency to be at a certain place at a certain time, I float. It's the procrastination issue.

Regarding Howard's Self-Understanding

Much like Diane, Howard was aware that he had problems with his ways of knowing and with meeting the expectations of others. His overall experience, however, was qualitatively different. Whereas Diane experienced a mixture of validation, invalidation, and neutrality, the composite described by Howard exuded a dearth of validation. Compounding the issue of having been raised in an invalidating environment was Howard's history of abuse, as well as having lacked any meaningful or lasting friendships as a child. Unable to reconstruct any experience before the fifth grade, Howard's recollections overwhelmingly reflected signs of habitual self-invalidation. According to Linehan (1993), self-invalidation occurs when an individual adopts the characteristics of the invalidating environment. No longer able to trust his own perceptions, he would rely on the perceptions of others. In other words, whether or not his self-assessments were accurate, Howard was well aware of the ways in which he failed to live up to the expectations of his parents, his teachers, his mentors, and (eventually) his wives. Although such persistence suggests a high incidence of self-monitoring, because his energy was so disproportionately spent looking for examples of failure, his efforts would have been unlikely to promote personal growth. Compounding Howard's fragile (and sometimes, volatile) sense of worth was that it hinged largely on a series of separate events (admittedly, within a history of self-devaluation). Following each event that turned out poorly for Howard, he would castigate himself. Given the quantity of undesirable events Howard has experienced, it has been difficult for him to reframe his pre-diagnosis experiences.

Unlike the others, even when Howard seemed able to navigate an obstacle, it seldom resulted in a newfound compensatory skill or strategy. Rather, many of his youthful attempts to tackle some task or to express himself led to a measure of defeat, sometimes catastrophic. Successive consequences led Howard's poor self-image to shield him from personal growth that may otherwise have been possible. Creating a book to report on was imaginative. That it happened the year he was held back served to frame it as a terrible lapse in judgment. Despite the adversity, Howard did seek ways of coping. Similar to Diane, Howard engaged in clowning behaviors as a way to draw attention away from poor classroom performance. In high school, clowning gave way to the delivery of amusing statements. Although they did not exactly roll off his tongue, these one-liners (as he called them) did provide him with a measure of pride. At minimum, he was aware of their positive reception.

Howard began to feel better about himself and his situation shortly before his diagnosis (the physical activity inherent in his soil-testing job being a good fit). Although he admitted having started on Ritalin "pretty much right away," he did not credit medication with his improved outlook. Howard's interview statements suggested that his level of self-awareness was firmly tied to his level of self-accep-tance. When feeling better, Howard has been more likely to suspend destructive self-criticism, a prerequisite for effective self-monitoring. Although his sense of possessing natural ability at the time of his interview series was considerably less pronounced than that of the other informants, he was able to discuss some recent gains. He acknowledged an ability to communicate more effectively, giving much of the credit to his experience teaching English as a second language (ESL). He was conflicted over his interest in professional advancement and the likelihood of being assigned to a desk (something to avoid). He cautiously described some abil-ity in helping learning groups to keep moving. Despite several poignant descrip-tions of his work with disadvantaged students, an underlying tone of not being able to do enough for them may have kept Howard from fully recognizing the contributions he has made. Then again, the sense of being unable to contribute anything meaningful to the world is common among adults with AD/HD (Brooks and Goldstein, 2006).

8

KARL:
"I would work laboriously each night."

At the time of our first interview, Karl was a thirty-four year old doctoral student who had not been formally diagnosed. I conversed with Karl via email for approximately six months, sensing a combination of interest and reluctance. I made it a point to wait for Karl's response to one message before sending another, and made it absolutely clear that this would be his decision alone. Based on diagnostic criteria from the DSM-IV-TR and several pages of my own experience as a point of reference, Karl concluded that he saw enough of himself in the material that he was willing to make a tentative self-diagnosis. Karl was filled with enthusiasm and spoke quickly. Despite criticizing his poor memory, Karl was able to recall many interesting examples that were rich in detail. About a third of the way into our first interview Karl said, "A lot of what I'm saying is only partly my own memory. It's also partly through conversations I've had many times with my parents over the years."

Experiences of Youth

One of the first things the reader is likely to notice is the comparative depth of Karl's youthful recollections. Given Karl's inability to sustain attention on schoolwork (in the classroom) and his obvious ability to concentrate when void of distraction (in private environments), I conceptualized Karl's formal learning experiences by adding a twist to Hartmann's (1997) *Hunter in a Farmer's World* analogy. To me, Karl often seemed to be a farmer on the wrong farm. [Karl's narrative begins.]

I had a lot of trouble in the school setting, because it was so incredibly difficult for me to focus. What always captivated me much more than anything the teacher said or more than anything I was doing academically was what was going on with all the other students. What were they doing? How could I get their attention? How could we laugh together? How could we secretly talk about something? Even just people watching: I would sit in a room with thirty other students and I would sit and just look at what they're wearing or how they're positioning their bodies. Not just whether or not there was a cute girl. It didn't matter. They all captivated me. I was a people person, so at any opportunity I tried to be humorous. I wanted to be the most likeable person, everyone's friend. More than one teacher called me the class clown.

I need to say one thing about thinking back as far as I can remember and that is my memory of my early years is quite horrible. I think the earliest that I can remember is kindergarten. I had a lot of traumatic issues associated with it and an inability to conform in the classroom. I also think that cognitively, I was pretty slow to develop. I couldn't see the big picture. I didn't really understand why I was in school or what school was for and when teachers said things to me, I took it as being one hundred percent honest. So when a teacher made a simple comment like, "You know, Mr. Mueller, if you don't do your work, you won't be able to play sports," I thought they were going to hold me to it and so I'd better do my work.

I remember I was always slow doing in-class assignments. One particular teacher got fed up with it and she said, "That's it, Mr. Mueller! You're going to stay here until you finish your assignments!" This was the last period of the day. In other words, school was ending. And when she said that, it put more stress on me to get it done and made it even harder for me to focus. Then the bell rang and the students went to their lockers for their coats. While they were putting on their coats, I was still stuck at my desk. Now I was worried that I was going to miss my bus home. This terrified me. I mean, I couldn't even think. If I couldn't concentrate before, now with everyone grabbing bags and walking around me, there's no way that I was going to be able to get this assignment done. This assignment was not going to happen. Students were walking out of the room. They were calling the first rows for the buses, and I hadn't even been to the lockers yet. I knew in my mind that no matter how much I had left, that I was not going to be able to do it. So I basically snapped. I stood up on my chair. I pointed my finger in the air and I remember screaming out, "I'm going to finish this once and for all!" And I screamed at the top of my lungs. Then the teacher said, "Yes, Mr. Mueller, you really do have a problem." It never occurred to me that if I stayed late, my parents would pick me up. I thought I was going to be trapped in that room all night long and it was a very scary thing to me. You can see this is some evidence that I was a little cognitively underdeveloped. Maybe a little bit insecure. Maybe a little bit frightened. All these things rolled together and affected my performance in the classroom. It was a really hard environment for me to work in.

After first grade, the teacher did not want to pass me on to second. My parents decided, actually through begging, that if they could get me ready for second grade over the summer, I would be allowed to move into second grade. So that summer and three or four subsequent summers my parents basically taught me everything that I should have learned in the previous grade. And invariably, by the time I hit the next grade, I was up to speed or even ahead of my fellow students, only to slowly, but surely, fall back behind by the following June.

I remember that I was by myself in a quiet room. We've always had a summer cottage that we went to with just my immediate family around. The cottage was such an important part of my development. My dad would wake up before me and have things set out with a list of what I needed to do each day. I wasn't allowed to go down to the beach or go outside and play until I was done. I was all by myself in the room. And because I was getting positive feedback, it was almost enjoyable. It was as enjoyable as something like that could be. I was seeing myself learn, and my dad would say, "See, you are learning. You're doing a good job." He was a very good role model. I'm sure I complained on the odd day, but it wasn't as burdensome as one might think. It was only a couple hours a day.

They would give me assignments to do, but without any instructions. Then they would go over it with me and say, "Look here. These three are wrong. Try them again." So I'd try them again. Then, "Okay. These two are still wrong. What are you doing wrong?" That's when they would give their instruction. I was required to be reading all the time too. Hardy Boys were my favorite books back then. That's what I did all summer long from the moment we got out of school until the moment we got back.

I don't know if it's relevant or not, but because of my difficulties in first grade—or maybe kindergarten—I had to go to a school psychologist for a couple sessions and be put through this battery of tests. The upshot was: they gave me the label of borderline learning-disabled, whatever that meant back then. They told my parents that one of the biggest difficulties I had was that I wanted to be perfect in everything and especially perfect in their eyes. I actually was a good kid and wasn't trying to misbehave or do poorly in school. I was almost trying too hard, and I was concerned about too many things. I was being distracted, not only by people in the classroom, but also by other issues like trying to be perfect in everything. All they said to my parents was, "We think he'll catch up. He's smart enough. He puts a lot of pressure on himself. You don't need to put any additional pressure on him. Just work with him. Support him. Help him and see what happens." Slowly but surely, things got better.

In second grade, I didn't know that teachers kept grade books. I looked around the room and I saw thirty-three other students and I said to myself, "There's no way that teacher would know if I miss an assignment I'm supposed to be doing in class." Actually, that was actually kind of intelligent thinking. I would take my papers and after signing them, crumple them up, drop them on the floor, and proceed to do nothing for a half an hour. I would rather not do it than sit there and try to work through an assignment. It was very hard for me to perform in the here-and-now classroom. Time testing just added more pressure, which made it more difficult for me to think and stay on target. Finally, at the end of the term, my second-grade teacher showed me a whole string of zeros in her grade book. You would think she would have told me after the first couple, but no. Then it dawned on me: Oh. She is keeping track. During time on the playground, I was totally crazy and being the class clown.

A lot of the confusion dissipated as I went into third and fourth grade. By eighth grade, I understood things fairly quickly and found that I was able to explain things to other students. That felt good. In other words, my ability to understand something quickly was always above average, while my ability to work on something and not be distracted was always well below average. Somehow, the two came together—I guess—and put me in the "B" group.

My parents weren't enamored with the parochial schools in our area so I went to a public high school where I was able to make friends quickly. There were a lot of people I liked and I was able to participate in a variety of sports. I had teammates, camaraderie, and a support network. I was amicable enough that everyone liked me and I liked everyone. That was a good thing. Quite honestly, I am also very observant when looking at subtle things that a lot of people miss. I seem to always pick up on a person's body language, their expressions, and how they're carrying on. Although, I probably worked harder at making friends than I did making grades. I was always goofing and playing even if the other students were paying attention. And this is something I do remember. This is why I think I am potentially a candidate for retroactive, self-diagnosis.

I would get interrupted by my thoughts, my dreams, my imagination, and my future. All of a sudden, twenty minutes would have gone by and I hadn't heard a word of what the teacher had said. I'd be looking at the teacher, but not a thought from what the teacher said would have entered my mind. I was off in la-la-land, but I didn't perceive it as la-la-land. I would be thinking about the way I'm swinging my baseball bat. I'd be thinking about a better way to shave some time off my stroke, in swimming. I'd be thinking about a woman I was attracted to and how I'd really like to meet her. I'd be thinking about the summers I had when I was younger. You know, just stuff. Clearly, it didn't even take other students to distract me. And if I was distracted for long enough and lost what the teacher had said earlier, it made it even harder for me to pick up what they were saying later. By the end of the class, I would give up. Maybe I knew what the teacher was saying for the first ten minutes of a fifty-minute class.

Somehow, I bought into the idea that I had the potential and I wanted to get good grades, so I would work laboriously on homework each night. The effort was partly because it took me longer to do the homework, the same rationale I gave for having to work during my summers. I would miss things. I would miss explanations. I would get part of it, but I wouldn't get all of it. It wasn't that I couldn't have understood it had I been listening. It was that I couldn't stay tuned in long enough. When it came to my homework, I had to go back and teach myself what I was supposed to have gathered that day in school, but things were better.

In high school, they kept you on target and you had to turn in the homework. Again, I bought into the idea that I couldn't miss any. I had to get these done. It might have made for some late nights, but by the time I went to bed, I was where all the other students were—right then—not just at the end of the year. I was starting to use textbooks as an important tool and found out that I was able to do well enough on homework by learning from the book and not from what the teachers said in the class. That's a learning strategy for sure because it helps me learn. It's coping too, because it's making up for what should have happened in class. I never let it bog me down too much. I truly believed that if I worked hard enough, learning from the textbooks, I could get the same end result that other students did.

Then something interesting happened. I started dating a girl back when I was fifteen. Fourteen? Fifteen? Maybe. I took my first class with her and she was sitting next to me. It was some math class. And all through the class I'm joking with her and finally she turned to me with fire in her eyes and said, "Can you do something for me? Can you shut up? Can you please shut up? Not only that—try this. Why don't you listen to what the teacher says and try to write down everything she says? Try it for one fifty-minute period. I dare you. Try it." So, I did. I remember gluing myself to what the teacher was saying. I had to work really hard at this because I was not very disciplined at it. I probably lashed out, but I had never consciously tried super hard to pay attention to the teacher.

I went home and an amazing thing happened that night. My homework took about a third of the time it regularly took because I remembered what the teacher had said and I had written down some examples from the board. It never dawned on me before that they actually told you how to do the homework before you got home. That never occurred to me. I always had to teach myself. I thought I had to learn from the examples in the book. So all of a sudden, it dawned on me that if you listen, it actually helps you. Duh. Right? And I was able to do that in my other classes too. And by and large, my grades jumped a whole grade level. She taught me how to play the game, how to tell what the teacher wanted. If they said this thing over and over, it meant that it would be on the test. These were things I never thought of before. Eventually I was able to settle down and figure out what I needed to do in the classroom each day, but because of my freshman and sophomore years, my overall grade point average was relatively low. So I went to community college.

Adulthood Experiences

Karl had become proficient at teaching himself. Despite the intensity of his study habits and the high marks he earned, he was still distracted by the physical classroom as well as by the seemingly random procession of thoughts that habitually appeared at inopportune moments. In his youth, Karl's discoveries helped him to learn. During early adulthood, however, his discoveries had much more to do with realizing his limitations.

It was at community college that I first started to get the inkling that maybe I wanted to become a college teacher. Because my grades were so good, I was able to get into a respected public university for my last two years. There, competition was wicked. Grueling. And I had to make up for lost time by working incredible hours. While other students would study twenty hours for a test, I might study for fifty. I was studying nonstop. I would wake up at eight in the morning and study straight through to ten at night—without so much as taking a break for lunch. I was a study maniac because I wanted to succeed. This worked well for me. A lot of people didn't want to go to a big university because of the huge classes where you can barely understand the professor—but I never relied on teachers to teach me. I was so distracted anyway, that I didn't get anything from the lectures. I was doing all of my learning out of the textbooks. Besides, I was maturing and taking pride in learning. I'm really happy to learn everything I can.

It was at that time that I started to realize other differences too. One of my courses was genetics and one of my study partners, Daniel, is now a metropolitan emergency room doctor. The problem was that Daniel got an "A" in genetics and I got a "B." And I firmly believe to this day that I understood genetic concepts as well as he did. I could get the same conclusions. I understood what was going on, but I couldn't operate as efficiently as he could. Every test I took in that course was twenty-five questions. I'd get to question twenty-one or twenty-two and time would be up. It was frustrating. It was then I started to see that I was clearly different from other people because I asked around. "Do you always finish?" "Oh yeah. There's always plenty of time for me to finish." I wondered, why was it that I was cogitating things more slowly? The same thing happened on the Graduate Record Exam. These weird memories would pop in my mind. I'd be thinking about a detailed problem, when all of a sudden, in a nanosecond, I'd be thinking about some fight I got into with my brother years ago. What the hell? Why am I in the middle of a test being interrupted with these thoughts and with this weird thinking? Something I read would make me think of something else and I would have to quickly divert my attention back on target. Do this one hundred times per test and it costs time. Consequently, I underperformed on many of these big tests, on anything timed, on anything where I felt pressure.

Caffeine would work to a point, but if I had too much it would create even more problems. I would start to see almost a caffeine plethora. When I didn't have enough I was slow at thinking and distractible. If I had a little bit, I could get to a good point where I focused well. If I had too much coffee then it seemed like I was beyond the point of no return and I went back to where I was all scatter-brained again. I would try to regulate it, but it was hard because there were some days that I had tons of caffeine and I thought great. Then there were other days that I didn't have the time to get coffee and I felt great too. Somehow the caffeine mingles with the stress or with how much you know the material or how competent you feel going in and it all comes together and at the end: here's how you're thinking today.

In graduate school, the courses were no longer timed and I found out that I actually did fine at gathering large amounts of information and retaining it for tests. Perhaps I didn't understand the bigger concepts as much, but I understood the genetics so I felt, man! I really do fit in and I can do this. Every time I succeeded in a science class that people viewed as hard, it slowly but surely built up my confidence as a learner. I knew that I wanted to be a community college teacher, and for the first year, I was hell-bent on trying to get a Ph.D. By the time I finished my master's degree I was absolutely burnt out and I took a teaching position at a technical college. I spent five years—ten—five years working there, from age twenty-six to thirty-one. During those five years, the dean said, "Karl, you know you have a lot of potential," many times. "You're young. You need to go for your doctorate." I was still reeling from that master's degree and would say, "That's not going to happen." Also, the financial incentive wasn't there. At my current job, however, they're very accommodating.

I did think of a story that's non-academic. When I was a graduate student, probably twenty-three—twenty-four—twenty-five years old, I took one year off and did volunteer social work out West. One summer my friend Richard—who I met while volunteering—flew out to meet me and my younger brother Tim and one of Tim's friends. The four of us were to embark on an eight-day, seven-night backcountry canoe trip in the Minnesota Boundary Waters. It was a wonderful experience. Now imagine for a moment that I took the responsibility of outfitting the entire trip. I rented a cheap motel room the night before we departed. We were all supposed to converge on this hotel room to bring all the gear together in one place. The degree of organization for this trip was pretty significant. We unloaded everything from my car and all the stuff Richard brought and it was strewn about the room. This small motel room had hundreds of hooks and fishing gear and fishing line and fishing poles and anchors and lifejackets and weights and paddles and food that had to be partitioned into little containers. There was stuff littering this room that you would not believe. I took pictures of the room. Then we went to work. Richard said, "Okay Karl, I'll take care of the food. Why don't you take care of getting all the fishing stuff organized?" So there I was, with everything littered all over the place. I started to get the fishing stuff organized, and this is how I knew that I was completely different from Richard.

I went to get the fishing line out of a bag and with the line was a mix that goes on the fish before cooking. Do I put this with the cooking gear or do I put this in with the fishing gear? And while I'm trying to decide that, I see my boots: the boots that I'm going to use in the canoe. Not at night. So I've got to make sure the boots go in the right bag. Wait. Where is that bag anyway? Then I go looking for the bag. Sure enough, I wouldn't be able to find it and I'd get all flustered.

When I finally did find it, I saw five other things on the way to get it that caught my attention that I wanted to be sure to do. I was spinning like the little swirl going down the drain. I was being sucked down, big time. We worked for about three hours. And do you know that I accomplished nothing at the end of those three hours? Richard had all the food done and had moved on to the clothes. He was just moving like a machine through this stuff. Finally, after three hours I said, "Rich." And you know what? He had to do everything that night. I was so useless. I actually went to the cooler, opened a beer, sat down and watched him pack. All I did while trying to pack was interrupt my own thoughts. I could never stay on task. And I thought to myself, wow. How completely different we are. It didn't bother me, because by this point I knew that something was going on all my life, yet I felt like I had done all right. I'm in graduate school. I'm doing all right. But clearly, can you imagine? That's what first gave me the thought to talk with my other brother who was already diagnosed with attention deficit. And he said, "That's exactly what would have happened to me. I would have been so scatterbrained because it's just too much." I was older and was never formally diagnosed with this disorder, but I know the way I learn and with the coping mechanisms or learning strategies I have—certainly there's a way that I'm different from some of the other people around me.

Considering Adult Education

Upon having made the decision to pursue a doctoral degree, Karl took a look around, sampled a few classes, and jumped right in.

I'd like to profess here that I did all sorts of research and that this program profoundly matches with me philosophically, but it's nothing that elegant. In fact, it comes down to sheer logistics: expediency, proximity, all the things that make it less of a hassle to do. That's not saying that I haven't been impressed with the people and the program. I actually have been. I'm probably more impressed than I expected in the beginning. Here's the interesting little part of the story. I actually didn't know the area in which I wanted to pursue a doctoral degree. I originally thought it would be neat to do something in science education, but didn't see that animal here. I guess I started taking exploratory courses more than anything else.

The first adult education course was a good course. I liked the professor and he was very approachable. I liked what he said, what he stood for, and I liked his approach to adult education. Soon, I started to become interested. He also kind of took an interest in me, saying, "Well, you think you like it. Let's get going. Let's get you applied. Let's get you through." He facilitated me through the process of getting in. And I've been very happy ever since.

The Graduate School Experience

In this segment, Karl's level of intensity becomes very apparent. Of particular interest are Karl's thoughts on what (adult) learning is *really* all about.

I've found that the professors in this adult education program are very broad-minded. They work very comfortably in the gray areas of the world. Not everything's black and white. That's different from my experience in the hard sciences. I've worked in environments where the professors or mentors had to break you down before they allowed you to develop. And that's not what I experienced in the adult education program here. I know that I'll have the legs kicked out from under me during the proposal process—but you can still get there. They're not trying to weed you out. They want to make sure that you can defend something, that you can believe in something strongly enough to carry it through.

I also like the structure of the program from a physical standpoint. I like that they hold classes in the city. While sometimes it irks me that I have to drive, the groups of students at each area are a little bit different. Moreover, it naturally broadens your horizons. You see all these people in the same program as you and they're not doing anything similar to what you are. Initially I had a very limited viewpoint of what learning was. I thought all we did in adult education was sit around while people gabbed. Once I was required to write reflection papers or to actually keep a journal, I suddenly realized I was learning a heck of a lot from these people. My fellow students were resources. Voila! There I was: sitting in a classroom at the downtown site and I have a firefighter, a police officer, people from the public schools, and people from the transit authority all sitting next to me. Now when I drive by the downtown site, I don't look at it as a big scary, ugly building. I look at it as a warm friendly environment where I've had a lot of good discussions and a lot of good memories. I've realized how the experiences I've had impact the way that I view the world and the way that it shapes my present and future learning. It's funny how we change. If I took all of my doctoral courses at the main campus, I would be less rich for the experience.

What the experience has drawn out of me is this whole understanding of society-at-large. In other words, I became way more sociological in my thinking, more worldly. I began seeing connections between power and class; I actually became transformed by my experiences in this sociological field. Because I had never been in this type of field before I really appreciated this new way of looking at things. I felt richer for it. When I think back to myself just coming through my master's degree, I see that I had tunnel vision. Science. Science. Science. Science had all the answers. Now I see that science is only one part of the greater context of life. Now I don't see the world so much as right or wrong. Because who's right and who's wrong? And why? Everyone is experiencing it differently. I mean—there are certain rights and wrongs that we can all agree on—the foundations, but there are people where it has to be this way or that way. It has to be a black or a white. Some people are actually quite frightened by a diverse world. They have their grounding that this is the way things are and this is how they're supposed to be and any variation from that causes serious stress, consternation, unpleasantness, and discomfort. And if you start to think about the world in a perverse manner, it's self-propagating. I'm right on the opposite: wanting to see things and understand things in a different way. I think that's somewhat interesting because this program has certainly allowed me to take a more broad approach to understanding the world. Then there are lots of times that you're like: oh boy. I don't know about this; or I don't know the right answers anymore. Sometimes you come up against the whole idea that the world is so complicated, people are so complicated, and we're so far into this, that who really knows anything? That's almost like a meltdown point where the world is too overwhelming. You get so far thinking of the world in a diverse, holistic, and idealistic way that all of a sudden it's hard to even understand people who have gone the other way.

One thing you have here is the experience of seeing yourself learn. I saw myself learn in a very conventional way in kindergarten through twelve, and again I saw myself learn in a very conventional way or at least in a scientific way through the master's program. You memorized great quantities of information and regurgitated it in a way that proved that you knew it or you were labeled as not smart. That was it. There was only one way to think. Once you learned it, you were done. And I truly identified myself as either smart or not simply on the grades I got and how I was performing in school, which, if you think about it, is such a limited way to identify yourself as either smart or not. Adult education has more epiphany-type learning, where all of a sudden you see the world in a different way. All of a sudden, you say, "Oh. I never realized this about the world in which I live." It's more of a realization type of learning rather than learning in which you memorize all the specifics that lead systematically to bigger things. I'm still learning in the sciences, but it's more factual. The learning I'm doing in the adult education program is just so much more. I'm not learning small stuff to learn more stuff. I'm hearing things in a new way that allows me to think in a way I've never thought before which allows me to understand and to go further. It's bigger learning. It's like an epiphany. And it happens in a lot of different ways.

Just sitting in the classroom with fellow students from different social or cultural backgrounds, different economic backgrounds. I can see myself changing, developing, and becoming a different person than I ever was before. Had I stayed in biology I would probably have retained that more narrow perspective.

I don't know. There's times when I'm in the middle of this program and I'm saying to myself, "I can't believe I'm doing this. How did I even get started?

What am I doing? I can't believe at this point in my life I'm actually doing this." Before, I just wrote it off. I think I've always dreamed big and I said to myself, "You know what? It'll be great to get my doctorate. It's a goal." It was always there under the surface of my skin and I think it just waited to jump out. You know? Then I thought, Yeah. Actually, it would be nice to do that. If they're good enough to get that degree, I could get the degree. All it takes is hard work, and the want, and the desire, and I can do that. And I don't know. Pride? I don't know what makes me do it.

I think I have a little bit to offer now that I'm in the midst of a doctorate program that I'll hopefully finish. I enjoy being in a situation where I don't know much, because I enjoy learning about stuff I don't know much about. This is probably one of my greatest enjoyments in life, just sitting around, maybe having a beer with a friend, and just talking about concepts like this. That's one of my greatest fascinations: to have these kind of intellectual conversations and just ponder and learn from each other. Some of my best friends are people who do this sort of thing with me.

Coping and Strategizing

Although Karl avoided assigning a definite meaning to the terms *coping mechanism* or *learning strategy*, he did mention them (at least in part). What he offered, however, was a number of compensatory behaviors that will likely remind the reader of Marianne, Diane, and Howard.

You think that as you get older that you're eventually going to stop behaving like a high school student, waiting until the last minute to do everything. I'm still waiting. Even in this doctoral program, I tend to wait until the last minute in everything. The procrastination thing is something I've never been able to circumvent. I've thought a lot about why I procrastinate and why other people, like my wife, don't procrastinate at all. Why is that? I have good intentions about getting things done ahead of schedule. I've found that my efficiency, my economy, is very poor when I have lots of time to do something. I find myself going into way too much detail and I'll get sidetracked within the project itself. I can't, you know, see the forest through the trees. I'll start a project and see something else that's interesting to read. Because I'm not under the gun, I'll take the time to read something that has nothing to do with the assignment; I'll search the Internet and I'll find something that's fascinating. Pretty soon an hour, two hours, three hours go by and I haven't gotten anything done on the project. In other words, I think my inability to stay on task is much worse when I'm not under pressure.

Contrast that with the night before something's due. I don't have any time to read anything else plus, I have a heightened level of stress: good stress. I'm energized. I'm concentrating. I've got to get this thing done. There's no time to fool around. I've got to cut through all the junk and find exactly what I need. All of a sudden, I'm able to work much, much more efficiently and quickly than if I had done the assignment earlier. And because many assignments are due around midterms or semester's end, everything stacks up and I'll have several deadlines within a week. So I work very productively—ferociously—even for extended periods. Even for weeks at a time. That's exactly how I operate. It's kind of all or none. I'll float along doing the minimum until it becomes a deadline. I don't do anything early. I always wait to the last minute. Whenever I've started something well ahead of schedule, I've worked at such a paltry pace that it would frustrate me and I would just put it off until the end. I think I've procrastinated all my life, yet I've never known why. After having taken the critical thinking class, it kind of came to me. Maybe this is why I procrastinate. Because it just takes too much darn energy when I'm not procrastinating.

I think the hyper-focus naturally kicks in when I feel that I'm running out of time. When I hit that wall where I go into critical mode, I actually treat deadlines as pretty serious things. A deadline is a deadline. I try not to procrastinate because it costs a lot in the end. Many times, I have to abandon my family for a couple of days. Not literally, but I can't help around the house. I don't use procrastination as a coping mechanism or a strategy. I always just naturally default to it, because there are always other things that I'd rather be doing when I'm working at a leisurely pace. So I think the conversation I'm going to have with my committee is whether they would hold me to task. Give me deadlines. Help me move along the program better. I don't know if they'll play that game with me, but I'm hoping they might.

There are times when I'm writing that I can't figure out what to say. Or I can't put the words together that accurately describe what I'm trying to convey. Guess what I do? I stand up. I walk around. I might jog a little bit. I'll come back and I'm amazed. Not that it will always work. There are times where it will come together after taking a short walk around the room. I've done this since high school, at least. I'll even type standing up. Walk around a little bit. Come back. Knock a sentence off or two while I'm standing. Walk around a little bit more. I don't know. I might even try it during exams. Maybe I'll ask for an area where I can stand or walk around—walk around, because I know that I operate better that way.

A Diagnosis in Doubt

Whereas each of the first three informants received official diagnoses of Attention-Deficit/Hyperactivity Disorder, Karl has never sought diagnosis. Because I lack the prerequisite licensure, and therefore, have no authority to render diagnosis, I make no attempt. Based on what I learned from Karl through our exchange of emails over a period of six months, I concluded that he would likely provide useable data. Obviously, this opinion has not changed. [Karl's narrative concludes.]

Let me qualify everything I'm going to say right now. Sometimes I have trouble constructing meaning when looking back. I just plow through life and if it's not an issue and doesn't bother me, I just keep going without ever thinking about it. Today, as I'm talking and making meaning as I go along, I've got to be able to stop and consider things. I think it's appropriate to start with my internal dialog in having decided to participate in this. One might think: oh, maybe you don't want to divulge personal information to a stranger, but it was not that. It really wasn't. The delay in the beginning was because I wasn't sure that I wanted to go through a formal diagnosis procedure at this point in life. I wondered how that would change my perception of myself. In some regards ever since I started hearing about this *disease*, especially since my brother was diagnosed, I've already begun to reframe my younger educational experiences in the context of, maybe ADD is the reason this or that happened. I thought that perhaps I could use it as a kind of opportunity to learn more about myself. Staring with the first interview, I was surprised by the things I said and by the realizations I was having. I've thought of some of those things a little bit before, but I had never spoken them aloud to anyone. When you speak things aloud, all of a sudden, you have different thoughts go through your head than when mulling things over while drifting off to sleep. Then, having your responses and your feedback and being able to have a dialog about it was something I had never done before. This is the first time I really started to explore this issue. It's not often in our lives that we're allowed to speak as freely and openly on something and having somebody be such a good and captive listener. It's a pretty gratifying experience.

Some people might be more reserved and not want to open up to others. I tend to not have those problems, but when you started to prod into how I think about myself as learner in this doctoral program, I started to realize one of the positives of this type of program. I think it is much more compassionate. It's more understanding and tolerant for people with varied learning styles. What I'm finding in the adult education program is that one person's strengths are another person's weaknesses and another person's mediocrities are where others excel. There are things that I'm really good at and things that I'm really poor at. What's important is that you can do what needs to be done even if it means getting help or assistance, or leaning on someone for help. I imagine that people I've perceived as brilliant in the hard sciences could be woefully lacking in some other area. I don't know why it never dawned on me that given our different backgrounds and cultures that we're as different as learners and as students as we are in anything else. Had I known that before, I don't think I would have been as hard on myself or would have been so pigeonholed in labeling myself as successful or not. I'm a person who does some things well. I also recognize what I don't do so well and try to head off some of those things. You just do the best that you can to the best of your ability with what you have, and you make it all work one-way or another.

Clearly, I've increased observations of myself as a learner. Maybe the way that I process or deal with things is different from the majority of people. That being said, there's a question I still don't have an answer to. If you went through this interview with one hundred and fifty different people, randomly chosen, might we all have unique educational experiences or areas where we have troubles with certain things? What I'm trying to ask is, am I just aware of myself more as a learner so that I am able to see myself better than other people? And does that kind of group myself in with AD/HD or whatever? Am I really different from the typical student with the way I'm thinking now? Or is it actually that we would all be different in our own little way and I just happen to know the little way that I'm different? Do you get my question? I don't know much about AD/HD, but the more I hear about it and the more I've read about and spoken to my brother about it, and with the information you've given me, it seems like I have some of those tendencies. Looking back, I really do have an experience that's a little different from the mainstream, but I have no concrete way of knowing. I'm not a clinician. I don't know enough about the tag actually. That was the bit of a hesitation getting into this interview process. I didn't want to waste your time. I don't think I would exclude a diagnosis of AD/HD. I think I have the whispers of it, or some of the tendencies or the flare-ups, or just a little bit of it. What I've read about AD/HD is that it doesn't really have a lot to do with intelligence. It doesn't mean you're dumb.

Regarding Karl's Self-Understanding

Through the majority of his youth, Karl did not judge his experiences as anything other than normal. As he matured, Karl learned about his idiosyncrasies through several eye-opening experiences he might refer to as epiphanies. During the final interview, Karl described the whole of adult education as epiphany learning, "where all of a sudden you see the world in a different way." Early epiphanies included the note-taking incident in high school and the realization that his undergraduate genetics classmates were not plagued by the intrusive, random thoughts he was. Whereas these experiences provided him with increases in self-understanding, they did not result in the development of specific compensatory behaviors as they did for Marianne, Diane, and to a lesser extent Howard. Rather, from an early age onward, Karl's primary compensatory learning strategy continues to be his ability to learn straight from a book. Complemented by being a quick study, Karl's confidence that ability and commitment would be enough to pull him through any educational challenge has been steadfast. Given the reliability of a select few learning strategies, an awareness of ways his specific set of challenges has served more as a point of interest than one of concern. Yet, Karl possesses a great deal of self-awareness and self-understanding. The crux is that his status as a scholar is not anywhere near as dependent on the high degree of self-knowledge required of the other informants, all of who had to rely on various combinations of coping mechanisms and learning strategies, each one addressing a relatively small portion of the overall equation.

Although any preponderance of doubt was not sufficient for him to decline participation, at the conclusion of our interview series Karl remained undecided as to his diagnostic status and seemingly reluctant to seek a formal evaluation. Having described his educational experiences as different from the mainstream, he questioned whether the differences might have had more to do with his heightened self-awareness than with the possibility of having AD/HD. Like Diane, Karl recognized the interview process as providing an opportunity to reflect on experience in unexpected and at times enlightening ways.

As a young boy, Karl had many unspoken questions regarding learning. Why was he in school? What purpose did school serve? Until his teen years, he had no idea what teachers did at the front of their classrooms. Nurtured from an early age, Karl's ability to teach himself prepared him for a protracted quest for knowledge that consumed the latter half of his undergraduate carrier, and it remained important thereafter. Through a succession of recent discoveries and epiphanies on the meaning of learning, Karl has come to embrace the far reaches of diverse thought. During his passionate dissection of what learning and education meant to him I envisioned Karl standing on a precipice of chaos and possibility, asking aloud, "How did I even get started?"

9

THEMATIC DISCOVERIES

Seidman (1998) suggested two basic ways to share data with others. The first option was to create profiles able to speak for themselves. The researcher could then augment these profiles through the identification of salient unifying themes. The second way was to organize excerpts according to theme alone, bypassing the profile and proceeding directly to analysis. In either case, the researcher was cautioned against the lure of any attempt to force-fit data into preconceived categories. Fashioning some combination of the two, also a suggestion, was my preference. The aim of this chapter is to identify and explore certain specific thematic connections leading to a synoptic presentation of essential meanings. Although a relative multiplicity of themes emerged, I did not select all for discussion. In addition to any themes of questionable strength, I ruled out themes emblematic of the *problem* of AD/HD. I grouped those selected for discussion into four primary categories: motivation, the impact of personal and societal interests, the impact of environmental structure, and the selective use of compensatory strategies. At the end of this chapter, I present seven essential meanings derived through examination of the themes discussed below.

Motivation

Unsurprisingly, the motivation to increase one's knowledge and effectiveness as a learner sprang from a variety of sources. Speaking broadly, external rewards and consequences were the most prominent motivators of childhood. With maturity came new sources of motivation. Although the influential power behind external motivators tended to decrease as internal sources of motivation increased, the relationship between external motivation and actionable response remained relatively constant. That is, throughout their formal education, the informants continued to be swayed one direction or another by various external motivators.

For three of the informants, specific external motivators led to avoidance behaviors. Recall Marianne's desire to deflect the nearly omniscient, critical gaze of the nuns who served as her educators, as well as her fear of stigmatization by classmates. Whereas Marianne went largely unnoticed in the classroom, Diane and Howard were routinely subjected to invalidation. In response, they devised intentional attention-seeking behaviors to distract their teachers from their unintentional ones. Being reprimanded for playing the role of class clown was much more desirable than being singled out for what felt like character assassination, especially given that it had to do with behaviors they scarcely understood and had little ability to control. In contrast, Karl's interest in clowning was without hidden motives. From an early age, both Diane and Howard learned—at times haphazardly—to fashion façades to distract others from inner conflicts that frequently rose to the surface despite ongoing struggles to keep them submerged. Although Karl also experienced a measure of fear and anxiety in response to certain teachers as well as to real and imagined repercussions, because of his inability to determine what was expected, Karl was largely unable to implement strategies to consciously avoid those consequences he found upsetting. Instead of responding to an avoidance-driven set of external motivators, once Karl learned how to identify teacher expectations, he found ways to meet them.

Even as the informants matured and became more self-assured, the essential natures of their external motivators have remained more or less consistent. The peer approval Marianne sought during high school, for example, is similar to the more recent concerns she described of tarnishing her professional image. With Diane, the need to prove her academic commitment to observant friends replaced her youthful need to prove her ability to the teachers who doubted her. Similarly, Howard's attempts as an undergraduate to disguise his lackluster note-taking ability has a parallel in his more recent efforts to keep a low profile during learning groups. For Howard, both behaviors served to camouflage his perceived differences from fellow students. Although his techniques have brought some success, Howard has continued to harbor anxiety over being discovered. When *smoke and mirrors* proved ineffective, especially in response to his sense of being a failure, Howard felt compelled to escape. As a youth, he longed to escape the confines of school. As a young man, he joined the Navy to escape his parents. As an adult, he has repeatedly sought emotional escape from the criticisms of his first, his second, and now his current wife. A clear factor in Howard's life has been his sensitivity to criticism and the bad feelings that have lingered well beyond each critical event.

Conversely, the majority of Karl's external motivators were positive. His father's praise served him well as a child. In college, high scores and good grades fed his scholarly ambitions. Most recently, the promise of a larger paycheck lured him back to school. Then again, the traditional motivators of financial compensation and professional advancement were in the minds of all. Emblematic of andragogical assumption, personal experience indicated to each that the time to continue their educations had come.

Although as a researcher I gave all information equal consideration, I must admit that examples of internal motivations were of far greater interest to me, personally. On one level, internal motivators were quite similar. Each recalled a number of personal interests that helped them connect to aspects of their respective school curricula as children. Diane loved art class. Howard became energized when the focus was on Native Americans or World War II. Sports kept Karl's attention. All four—especially Marianne—described some level of interest in reading.

These early factors notwithstanding, the most significant outgrowth of generalized internal motivation, as noted by Latham and Latham (1997), was the result of simple maturation—something mentioned by all four. When Marianne made the decision to complete her bachelor's degree, for example, she described herself as so much more ready to be in school. Apart from any external reward, Marianne also claimed a willingness to persevere simply to satisfy her want of accomplishment.

Having described her childhood community as small-minded, Diane saw college as an opportunity for intellectual growth. What began as an externally motivated drive to prove her intelligence led Diane to envision herself as a more capable teacher than her teachers had been. In essence, what began as an attempt to prove something to others became a quest to validate her transformed self-understanding. Years later, armed with an awareness that there were many ways to be intelligent, Diane's maturation and successes as a learner served to promote a rise in self-confidence. This rise had a direct, positive impact on her sense of internal motivation.

Once enrolled as graduate students of adult education, three of the informants described features of their program as having motivated them toward continued learning. Although not specifically identified as a source of motivation, Howard's relatively flat affect during his series of interviews did give way to increased tonal vitality during his discussion of favorable elements within his master's program. For Karl, the greatest source of internal motivation came from the realization that he had found his life's calling: adult education. Nevertheless, Karl also admitted to having occasional lapses in motivation, not in terms of learning, but in response to a longing to return to the lifestyle of a husband, a father, and a friend. Given Karl's driven personality, it could be that he has not allowed himself enough down time. Whereas intentional periods of non-productive activity (or perhaps, inactivity) may help to rejuvenate the individual, Hallowell (1995) observed that mindlessly surrendering to cognitive dysregulation is likely to exacerbate one's symptoms of AD/HD. Like Marianne's parting assertion that she could not see her quest for knowledge ever coming to an end, Karl's final thoughts affirmed his unwavering thirst for conversations where the goal is mutual enlightenment. Such attitudes toward knowledge acquisition seem to parallel Ratey's (2001) contention that a passion for learning should pave the way for talents to flourish and minds to maintain their health.

Some of the time, internal motivators were readily identifiable. At other times, they were less apparent. Although Marianne's intrinsic drive to know more, to do more, and to keep learning no matter what was proclaimed with the most vigor, everyone described a strong need to know and an overriding belief in their ability to succeed, regardless of obstacles or evidence to the contrary. Diane declared, for example, that determination was a part of her character and that she possessed a willingness to complete a given task no matter what the cost. Similar to Diane's eventual self-acceptance of admittedly unconventional ways of knowing as valid, Howard returned to college to see if he could do better. By midlife, Howard came to believe in his potential. Unfortunately, where his potential would lead remained a mystery for many years. Uncertain as to its origin, Howard began to imagine himself as an educator and when the opportunity arose, he gladly welcomed it.

Beyond Karl's ability to learn in isolation, it was his depth of determination that unified and ignited his collective strengths. Assuming Karl does in fact have AD/HD, his remarkable success with a singular learning strategy has put him in the minority, as many highly proficient students with AD/HD tend to have a variety of strategies at their disposal. Common wisdom is that those who rely upon the rigid application of a single method are more likely to be underachievers (Sandler, 1995). Illustrative of the effect of domain mastery, Karl was resolute in his belief that a combination of high grades and having witnessed himself learn provided the lion's share of his motivation. Nevertheless, he did recall that sometime before second grade a school psychologist recognized the depth of his determination as well as his focus on perfectionism. Despite wide differences in levels of self-efficacy, the common thread between the experiences of Marianne, Diane, Howard, and Karl was that none were able to pinpoint the impetus for their underlying drive to learn. This is not a particularly uncommon experience, however, as Maxfield (1989) observed, a person's capacity for learning often far exceeds their full cognizance of it, as well as their ability to describe it.

Of particular personal interest was what I have termed "symptom-triggered motivations," defined as motivators resulting directly from the lived experience of a given symptom. I discovered several examples within the transcribed interviews of Marianne, Diane, and Karl. Examples from Marianne were rooted in her experiences with distractibility and impatience. The reader may recall Marianne's description of people-watching. More than a simple distraction, Marianne would ask herself a series of questions as she studied each person. Despite the unlikelihood of such a habit to yield much in the way of useful information, Marianne's seeming distracted gaze belied a strong sense of curiosity and offered a glimpse into the degree to which she was willing to direct her consciousness toward satisfying it.

I identified Marianne's other noteworthy symptom-triggered motivation as impatience. Midway through our third interview, Marianne mentioned that she was having difficulty concentrating and placed the blame on a meeting scheduled for later that afternoon. Easily irritated by drawn-out discussions, Marianne has been able to harness her impatience as a means to find solutions.

Previously, I discussed determination as an intrinsic motivator. Interestingly, for Diane and Karl, especially, the depth of their determination has often hinged upon the length of their procrastination. The AD/HD literature frames procrastination as an unintentional behavior. Indeed, when questioned about the link between his experience of procrastination and hyper-focus, Karl stated that he did not consciously use procrastination as a learning strategy. Whether allowing tasks to pile up entails a deliberate act of avoidance, the result is the same. As some impending deadline approaches, an otherwise dull task can transform into a highly stimulating one. As it happened, the longer Diane, Karl, and/or Marianne procrastinated, not only would their depth of determination be greater, but they would also become more effective, attaining higher benchmarks of scholarship. Instead of being more likely to make careless mistakes when short on time, they were, in fact, less likely.

Impact of Personal and Societal Interests

It would be fair to suggest that commonalities among underlying values and societal concerns played at least some role in choosing a graduate program in adult education. A much stronger argument would be that these commonalities served to affirm their choices after acceptance into their respective programs.

Initial reasons for entering graduate school ranged from the pragmatic to the visceral and generally contained elements of each. Having graduated high school in 1971, Diane cited the teaching profession as being one of the few options readily available to women. Regardless, Diane had deeply personal reasons for entering the field. Although Marianne's view of what was possible was virtually limitless, she too felt compelled to enter teaching. The primary difference between the two involved the wherewithal to identify the impetus for their decisions. Diane was able. Marianne was not. Howard and Karl were both able to provide some rationale for their interest in teaching, yet their decisions seemed more dependent upon the conceptual flip of a coin than contemplation. As Howard put it, the idea of becoming a teacher grew on him like a mushroom. Whatever meaning the mushroom analogy held for Howard, he did express a long-standing interest in issues of social justice and had the life experience to support his assertion.

Of the four, Diane's sense of altruism was the most visible. Having had to overcome so much adversity (AD/HD, dyslexia, problems with hearing and speaking clearly, and a certain fragility with self-acceptance) fed her sense of mission to help others do likewise. Yet, regardless of the specifics that brought the informants to their respective programs, all described a high regard for the philosophic underpinnings of adult education. Marianne discovered a completely new body of information to gleefully explore. Diane saw that everyone had a stake in shaping the learning process. Howard remained committed to teaching special needs and ESL. In response to his transformation concerning how he has come to understand learning and knowledge, Karl began applying his newfound and interconnected vision of academia to his classroom curricula, crediting the "sociological perspective of adult education" as his prevailing source of motivation. The apparent impact of their respective adult education programs seems to parallel a description that Smith, Roland, Havens, and Hoyt (1992) gave of challenge education (a contextual form of education where learning is interwoven with physical and perceptual challenges). A benefit of participation in such programs, they affirmed, is that individuals are able to form a clearer idea of who and what they (as well as the human community) may yet become.

Impact of Environmental Structure

Similar to the shared perception of formal adult education programs being responsive to issues of social justice and welcoming of diversity was an appreciation for what Howard described as a loose-knit, organized core, around which learners were able to individualize their program. Having expressed a general fondness for inclusive environments and program flexibility, each remained cognizant of how their symptoms (or *characteristics*, for Karl) of impatience, distractibility, and/or procrastination were ready to materialize when given too much freedom or time. Just shy of this threshold, the informants all seemed to thrive. Once crossed, however, each would experience a sharp descent into a state of decreased learner effectiveness.

In contrast to her youthful reliance on the parochial school structure, Marianne offered the most overt praise of the flexibility of graduate school. The reader may recall Marianne's certitude that the persistent sameness of a cohort program would have driven her crazy. Preferring elasticity, Marianne's rave regarding the scholarly freedom to think as she pleased in the classroom was in vivid contrast to her frustrations over the hierarchal systems present in her office. Perhaps her self-described logical, concrete way of thinking served to offset the absent, unyielding external structures she relied upon as a youth, and so vehemently has resisted as an adult. Clearly, the stronger her need to identify the problem and implement the most workable solution, the greater force her internal structure is able to wield. Having thus railed against inflexible environments, there was some irony in Marianne's experience of being unable to make progress on her research project when given too much freedom. This irony is somewhat common, as even highly intelligent individuals with AD/HD who have managed the complexities of their symptoms—sometimes reach a symptom-related barrier (Biggs, 1995). Barriers that emerge suddenly are most likely to occur in the workplace or institutions of higher education (Nadeau, 1995). For Marianne, there was one undeniable structural element necessary for her to maintain her effective edge: a time limit. In fact, when given too much personal responsibility for the creation of a timeline, all the informants struggled—all four having admitted a long-standing habit of waiting until the last possible moment before starting task.

For Marianne and Howard, program flexibility had much to do with the types of courses they were able to pursue. Karl was impressed with how well his program enhanced what he was doing in the field of biology education. For Diane, however, program flexibility meant a learning environment where individual learning styles were accepted and valued. In a setting where professors actively put theories of adult education to use, Diane learned to evaluate and appreciate her learning styles. In this respect, her professors modeled an element of self-regulated learning for the observant student. Diane pointed out that her experience with adult education was that the individual was encouraged to incorporate whatever worked best. In just such an environment, Diane's level of self-acceptance has grown. Her only disappointment was in response to the apparent rigidity of her program's doctoral candidacy exam.

Of the four, the impact of program flexibility was perhaps the greatest on Karl. Although all three of the doctoral students described a sense of feeling driven, Karl's descriptions exuded a level of intensity one could describe as frenzied: eat, sleep, study, and attend class. Karl spoke quickly, often blurring one word into the next. He also described his competition as an undergraduate as wicked and grueling. Apart from periodic bursts of intensity, Marianne had a much more relaxed way of expressing herself. She spoke more slowly, used a softer voice, and paused more frequently. In terms of his conception of graduate school, it was clear that Karl's doctoral experience represented a significant departure from his master's experience, which he described as militaristic. Initially, Karl was not quite ready for the student-centered learning environment of adult education. It took the task of keeping a reflective journal before he was able to reframe the free-form communication occurring in some of his classes as a potential wellspring of knowledge. Karl found this dynamic to be most apparent while taking off-campus classes in an otherwise foreboding urban area. He also recognized that challenges thrust upon him were not to break him. Rather, they served to ascertain the strength of his intellectual commitment. Like Marianne and Diane, Karl came to recognize his fellow students as resources. Similarly, Howard realized that he had something to learn from his at-risk students.

A final point of interest regarding the learning environment had to do with issues of distraction. Whereas visual stimulation can easily capture the interest of the AD/HD brain without undue stress (much like a daydream can), auditory stimulation can have quite the opposite effect. Random auditory stimuli (such as distant conversations, the chirping of insects, the hum of fluorescent lighting, and/or other irrelevant stimuli) are more likely to breed annoyance. Furthermore, when stimuli compete, it can be difficult to sort the important from the unimportant. In response, one's focus can jump back and forth between sources. Although this aspect of the learning environment did not generate much discussion overall, at least one distinct difference was voiced. Although both Karl and Marianne recalled instances, in which they were the cause of someone else's distraction, only Marianne found it politically necessary to isolate herself in response—even though she found background noise helped her to concentrate. For Karl, isolation was all about keeping external distractions at bay.

Compensatory Strategies

I read the central question aloud at the start of each interview. As mentioned, this question underwent a series of revisions as the research progressed. While still in the data collection phase, the terms *coping mechanism* and *learning strategy* (though eventually discarded) remained a distinctive part of the question. Consequently, each informant heard me refer to the set of terms on at least three occasions. Aware that people often use terms imprecisely, I kept my working definitions private. This awareness also kept me from absentmindedly assuming that I knew what each informant meant when using some variation of either term.

Initially, my understanding of each was quite loose. Upon realizing the folly of pursuing research without full cognizance of what my question actually asked, I set about finding their definitions. With the *Oxford English Dictionary* (OED) as my source, I could find neither—rather, their definitions would need to be constructed. For this task, the OED was the perfect tool. I came to define *coping mechanism* as a deliberate action or process through which an individual is able to temporarily manage or relieve a known, recurring obstacle, resulting in a short-term increase of satisfaction. My definition of *learning strategy* solidified as a sustainable approach whereby an individual is minimally able to maintain an initial increase or refinement in the knowledge acquisition process. Finally—during analysis—I settled on the single term: *compensatory strategy*, defined as a deliberate and sustainable approach enacted for the specific intent of reducing or offsetting unpleasant or unwelcome effects.

Printed Material

In series of interviews, the informants raised the subject of self-help books. For each, the reaction was similar. Marianne was surprised to discover that what the books she read had to offer consisted largely of techniques she had figured out on her own. Around the time of Marianne's diagnosis, Hallowell (1995) postulated that much of what should prove to be some of the most useful information concerning AD/HD had yet to make the journey from the minds of those with AD/HD to the printed page. This is not to say that such books were not helpful in some ways. They were—especially with regard to the concrete, real-life examples drawn from the experiences of others. For Diane, the sense of community such books provided was more valuable than the actual tips or techniques. [Her comment about losing her "to do" lists was reminiscent of my own thoughts on the subject of such tips: having to perfect someone else's suggestions designed to keep me on track is just another layer of *stuff* separating me from actually getting started.] Diane also mentioned having visited on-line sites for similar reasons and with similar results. Howard's outlook was one of simple skepticism.

Over the period of several months during which Karl debated whether to participate in this study, he claimed to have done some research on the topic of AD/HD in hopes of gaining a broader understanding. It is perhaps nothing more than speculation, but given Karl's reliance on book learning, it could be argued that he is the most likely of the informants to incorporate any of the advice contained within such publications. Clearly hesitant about seeking a clinical evaluation, the value Karl found in anything he read on AD/HD was in terms of reassurance. Having read that AD/HD does not impinge one's intelligence clearly provided him with a sense of relief.

<u>Stimulants</u>

In place of stimulant medication, many adults (with AD/HD) choose to self-medicate through caffeine, sometimes to considerable excess (Amen, 2001). Diane discovered that she enjoyed drinking coffee in the morning around the same time as her strong showing on a high school intelligence test. During Diane's first interview, she made the claim that caffeine had a tranquilizing effect on her and that if she drank too much she would get sleepy. She observed that the calming effect produced by coffee has proven especially helpful during meetings and other situations in which remaining seated has been the expectation. Following diagnosis, Diane tried an assortment of different prescription medications, but was unable to find one that met her needs. Whereas one medication helped her to focus, she built a tolerance for it and felt uncomfortable with the thought of having to take increasingly larger doses. Ritalin (perhaps the most well-known medication used to treat the symptoms of AD/HD) simply had no noticeable effect for Diane. After trying different medications Diane decided to forgo the treatment and instead "started stepping up with the coffee." When the subject of medications came up with Marianne, she stated that she did not have anything against medication, but essentially dismissed the idea by emphasizing the success she has had in the development of an array of compensatory strategies. Unlike the other informants, Marianne did not mention any use or reliance on caffeine.

Howard sought an evaluation shortly after his eldest son was diagnosed with AD/HD and with encouragement from his parents and ex-wife. Upon diagnosis, he began taking Ritalin. He has since taken one dose of Ritalin every morning and has taken up to two additional afternoon doses depending on the amount of work that he has to perform. On those occasions when he has forgotten a dose, he has taken something with caffeine in it. Howard's understanding of Ritalin has been to see it as a way to open doors to opportunity that would not have been accessible before. At the time of the interviews, Howard was the only informant currently taking prescription medications to address the symptoms of his AD/HD.

Although he did not link his use of caffeine specifically to the long hours spent studying, what is noteworthy in Karl's case was his struggle to achieve just the right balance. Where the right amount helped him to focus, what constituted the right amount would vary. Sometimes it involved "tons" of caffeine. At other times such a quantity would lead to Karl feeling "scatterbrained." If, indeed, Karl has AD/HD, attempting to find just the right balance of stimulant usage makes perfect sense.

<u>Vocalizations</u>

Apart from any discussion of AD/HD, Furjanic and Trotman (2000) noted that speaking aloud while engaged in learning activities is characteristic of auditory learners in general. Of the informants, it was Marianne, Diane, and Karl who had something to say about vocalizations as a learning strategy. Marianne's first example addressed why it was better for her to work on high school math assignments alone, in which she said, "For some reason, vocalizing is really helpful to me." As a doctoral student, Marianne mentioned that she has read aloud to herself when the assigned articles have been too dense. In addition to their verbosity, feelings of boredom would often complicate her task. The reader may recall the strong influence of boredom in Marianne's bouts with decision-making. Certainly, anyone who has endured a particularly boring afternoon knows all too well the seeming impossibility of getting to a task, even when there may be some promise of becoming energized. Although not specific to persons with AD/HD, Sandler (1995) observed that persons with attention deficits often come to the end of a chapter, or entire book, only to discover that they zoned out and have little to no idea of what was just read.

Similar to Marianne's strategy of highlighting what she has read (given her apparent status as an auditory learner), one could easily imagine how hearing what she sees would likely aid her depth of comprehension—a technique suggested by Parente and Anderson-Parente (1991). While it is clear that she used vocalization as a way to help her to maintain focus, she also mentioned the habit of speaking aloud when talking is not the norm or when people nearby are trying to concentrate. Despite the educative benefits Marianne has personally derived from giving voice to her thoughts, when others have been involved, Marianne's habit of incessant talking has hampered some of her professional relations.

Diane's experiences were perhaps less significant as a compensatory response to her symptoms of AD/HD. The reason Diane shared for saying words aloud had to do with her inability to hear sounds accurately. By saying words aloud, she has been able to better reproduce pronunciations correctly.

The role of vocalization in Karl's learning became apparent to him through the course of my interviewing him. He expressed surprise at some of the things he said and at the sudden realizations he made. According to Karl, one such realization was, "When you speak things out loud, all of a sudden, you have different thoughts go through your head than when mulling things over while drifting off to sleep." Having defined the realization as a new discovery, it was questionable as to whether or not vocalizations had previously played any compensatory role.

Hyper-Kinetics

Symptomatic of AD/HD, fidgeting and squirming may also be characteristic of kinesthetic learners (Furjanic and Trotman, 2000). In discussion of the learning needs of school-aged children, Armstrong (1994) used the term hyper-kinetic to describe the act of using one's whole body to express ideas or feelings. These conclusions aside, consider DSM-IV-TR (2000) criteria (a) for hyperactivity, which states the individual often fidgets with hands or feet or squirms in his or her seat. Recall Marianne's statements regarding her constant movement and how it helped her to concentrate. In essence, Marianne's symptom of hyperactivity has proven useful to combat her difficulty with sustained attention: criterion (b) for inattention. Nevertheless, one might be tempted to describe the hyperkinetic act of a diagnosed person getting up from his or her seat and walking around, especially when paired with vocalizations, as an example of someone exhibiting multiple symptoms. According to Linksman (1996), however, walking while talking may constitute an ideal learning situation whether or not any "symptoms" are involved.

Diane learned, or coped, by mixing study time with short walks around the house, by stopping to clean up a mess, or by hopping onto her exercise bike—suggesting an ability to think fast while on the go.

Karl's experience of using hyperkinetic movement began during high school and has continued through the present. For Karl, bodily movement has helped him to overcome writer's block, from high school through the present. He spoke of walking around, jogging, and even typing while standing. Karl used his predilection for movement as a learning strategy and possibly as a coping mechanism. Aware of the role movement has played in stress reduction during timed examinations, Karl voiced an interest in asking his professorate whether he might be allowed to get up and walk around the room while taking his doctoral qualifying exam.

The role of movement in Howard's ability to cope was less pronounced, yet unquestioningly present. Emphasis in his case rested upon the recognition of a need to stand up and move around. Citing this bit of self-knowledge, he expressed mixed feelings about applying for a desk-job for which he might be qualified. Having contemplated the very same dynamic, Marianne had already refused to seek a higher post within her workplace, as the position would require her to attend more meetings. Sitting still for long periods was not Marianne's strong suit. Similar to the shared experience of the informants, Weiss (1996), who has AD/HD, shared that standing or moving around while conversing has helped to focus her attention. In addition to the helpful role that physical activity has during periods of learning, regular exercise is valuable to persons with AD/HD, in general (Amen, 2001; Hallowell, 1995).

Hyper-Focus

In contrast to a widespread notion that individuals diagnosed with AD/HD are unable to direct or sustain their attention with much discernable reliability, clinical observations have pointed to the ability of most to engage sustained concentration during certain tasks or in specific situations (Brown, 1995). Although not a technical term, hyper-focus (or *hyperfocus*) has been used to describe an apparent benefit of AD/HD: the ability to focus with great intensity on a particular task for prolonged periods. It is not that the individual with AD/HD lacks the functions associated with sustained attention. Rather, it is that these functions do not respond to willpower alone (Brown, 2000).

Beyond whether or not the phenomenon of hyper-focus (or *hyperfocus*) is an asset to the AD/HD mind, the malleable nature of the term can breed confusion—just as Professor Ilsley had warned. To this effort, I assembled a working definition for each variant. I defined "hyper" as meaning hyperactive, excitable, highly-strung, and/or extraordinarily energetic. It can function both as a separate word and as a prefix. As a prefix, hyper can appear with or without a hyphen. When hyphenated, it serves as a qualifier to heighten the position of the second element and in the process loses much of its separate intensity. When used without a hyphen, however, the intensity remains intact. I defined "focus" as the center of activity or area of greatest energy. Prefixed with the hyphenated form of the word *hyper*, the term *hyper-focus* implies that the center of activity or area of greatest energy is approached in a way that exceeds expectation. Lacking hyphenation, the term *hyperfocus* describes a phenomenon in which an individual approaches the center of activity or area of greatest energy in an excitable, highly strung, and/or extraordinarily energetic way. Despite the self-help literature's apparent preference for the non-hyphenated form, I prefer using hyper as a prefix so as not to diminish the meaning of the word, *focus*.

Upon enrollment, Marianne's plan was to limit her self to one course per semester, but shortly thereafter, enrolled in two or three courses concurrently.

Had she not increased her course load, Marianne feared that she would have lost her momentum, which would have made it difficult for her to remain focused over the long term. If in fact, this were an example of hyper-focus, it would have been by far the longest period of continuous, focused effort of the four. Regardless, this paradigm paralleled numerous, lesser examples, such as incidents in which Marianne would frenetically dismiss any suggestion unlikely to produce a workable solution in her rush to move to the next situation. With regard to prolonged periods of such focus, Karl's experience most closely rivaled Marianne's, with his description of periods of ferocious productivity that could last for weeks. Dependent on the nature of the task and the individual's level of interest, the length one is able to focus can be measured in months, as well as weeks. Karl's experiences also involved both short and long periods of hyper-focus. Whether prolonged, or fleeting, Karl equated the phenomenon with what he termed "good stress." In other words, he found it to be effective. For Howard, periods of procrastination could trigger the ability to remain on task, even over a period of days. Like Marianne, Howard described a kind of aimlessness when lacking some sort of a schedule (supplied from the outside) for larger tasks.

Comparable to Karl's "good stress" was the apparent, anxiety-induced adrenalin rush Diane often depended upon to get started on a project. And comparable to the ferocity Karl described was Diane's following string of statements: "Determination is just part of my character. If there's something I need to do, I will persist at it if it kills me. That means I may get a migraine. I may not have sleep. I may stay up all night. If that is what I have to do to get the assignment done, I do it."

Universal to the informant experience (as well as to my own) was a particular theme within a theme. I believe that Karl stated it best, having said, "I don't do anything early. I always wait until the last minute. I think the hyper-focus naturally kicks in when I feel that I'm running out of time."

Humor

Besides the more obvious benefits of humor, such as simply having a good time, humor also helps to offset "burnout" when burdened with stress (Weiss, 1996). For Diane and Howard, humor played just such a role. All but Marianne recalled having purposefully set out to draw attention to themselves as children through humor. Whereas Karl found clowning as a way to get the attention of his classmates, for Diane and Howard, it served more to draw attention from their deficits. For Diane it resulted in a combination of laughter and reprimand. Howard discovered that although his pranks often led to adverse outcomes, a well-placed joke could help him to gain some measure of acceptance among his peers (and at times) his teachers. In contrast to the other three, Marianne spent her time in class largely unnoticed. Although she did not cite the use of humor as a compensatory or learning strategy, she did present herself as a light-hearted person during our interviews. Although I shared moments of levity with all four of the informants, the transcript shows that the most laughter occurred during interviews with Diane—the person who identified laughter with learning.

While discussing her experience of an adult education class that focused on the use of humor in education, Diane had an epiphany: that she has used humor as a learning strategy, rather than simply as a coping mechanism. When experiencing difficulty grasping a concept or simply being able to concentrate, Diane looked for ways to interject humor. Not only has the resulting sense of levity proven helpful to Diane as a means to cope, it has provided her with an unexpected learning strategy. So long as she is able to remember the joke, she is also able to remember the piece of knowledge connected to it.

Synopsis: Presenting the Essential Meanings

Respecting my research method, I limited thematic connections to what was observable within the transcripts. Having done so, I fully expect that the content of this chapter was consistent with any observations a reader might make. I understand that some conflict may yet arise in response to the visibility I gave certain themes over others. Then again, as a qualitative researcher, one of my goals is to encourage further questioning and critical thought. From the four primary themes explored in this chapter, seven essential meanings emerged.

1. Before diagnosis, the informants experienced unexplained (or inaccurately explained) learning difficulties and were able to find ways to compensate with limited assistance from teachers, parents, or self-help books.

2. Each had a persistent internal source of motivation and an awareness of a personal threshold beyond which they were likely to succumb to an unknown quantity of symptoms.

3. Increased self-awareness led to both increased positive and negative self-perceptions.

4. The ideals of social justice and respect for diversity were highly regarded, and served as a vehicle for motivation.

5. Elements of each of the adult education programs were pivotal in terms of improved self-understanding and heightened self-acceptance.

6. To varying extents, each relied upon a range of behaviors (commonly referred to as symptoms of AD/HD) to increase their ability to navigate formal education systems, as well as simply to learn.

7. In some cases, behaviors symptomatic of AD/HD played a useful role in combating other behaviors symptomatic of AD/HD.

10

NAVIGATION OF THE GLASS MAZE

Qualitative research places its emphasis on having looked at a problem in a particular way. In this study, the phenomenon in question has been as central to my set of experiences as it has been to those of the informants. That is, we were all graduate students of adult continuing education programs diagnosed with (or plausibly identified as having) AD/HD. I deliberately explored my own set of experiences before conducting any of the interviews. This step served two vital functions. First, it helped acclimate me to the research method I chose. It also provided a format for the reader to gain some understanding of how I managed my own AD/HD, as well as having provided a context for the reader to assess my credibility. Had I chose not to confide with the readership, any of my conclusions could be viewed with skepticism.

Starting with the first read of the first transcript, acts of interpretation have been nearly constant. As I had to consider all passages equally, my first step was to identify those of possible significance, with all doubts deliberately erring on the side of inclusion. Whereas I could easily discard anything insignificant, off topic, or repetitive later, the careless omission of some statement of significance early on could jeopardize the discovery of an important theme. Consequently, I vigorously maintained vigilance.

The selection process involved consideration of each separate statement on its own merits. Had I sought only those passages that seemed to tell a coherent story, the integrity of my study would already have fallen victim to an agenda. Besides, storytelling was not my goal. Just as previously held assumptions had to be cordoned from analysis, I had to resist the lure of crafting profiles before all the interviews were complete. Otherwise, the details of one person's story might have inadvertently influenced the story of another. Fortunately, the chronological structure of in-depth interviewing helped to block many of my distracting thoughts regarding presentation style at a time when active, empathic listening was my most important task. Once I selected the passages, I revisited the question of significance. Satisfied that I had removed the irrelevant, my role of interpretation shifted from seeking significance to searching for internal connectivity.

Achieving an accurate chronology, however, turned out to be a surprisingly arduous task. Many individual statements included a collage of memories as informants struggled to convey tangles of thoughts, experiences, and emotions in a limited amount of time.

Nevertheless, my perseverance was rewarded. Once completed, each profile had the advantage of being able to "speak" for itself. By "listening," I identified and explored thematic connections found within and between them. Lastly, I culled the essential from the extraneous, which led to the synoptic identification of essential meanings—satisfying the phenomenological task. Having met the methodological goal, what remained was my desire to place these meanings within a greater context. To this end, I shall evaluate my initial set of guiding assumptions, highlight a number of noteworthy surprises, address my own critical self-examination and revisit the central question. Thereafter, I will re-present the essential meanings in an accessible, reader-friendly format.

Preexisting Assumptions

Regardless of whether or not one is able to convincingly suspend a majority of one's assumptions, it would be disingenuous to claim that assumptions do not exist. In recognition of this, it is important for the researcher to identify them and to comment on the extent to which the data supported them. Early in the first chapter, I outlined two assumptions regarding certain qualities of graduate students of adult education.

My first concerned the nature of such students and their ability to provide insightful commentary on the role that self-understanding plays in response to, and in management of, AD/HD. It is true that my thoughts regarding their scholarly character and what they had to offer provided a great deal of personal motivation leading toward this study. That I stated my assumptions so early in this dissertation should help to affirm the transparency that has been central to my efforts. Indeed, embedded within the informant profiles of Marianne, Diane, Howard, and Karl, I found many examples of self-understanding playing a role in response to and in management of the informants' AD/HD.

My second assumption addressed graduate students' scholarly inclination for critical thought and the methodological expertise to examine the self-as-learner. As we know, critical inquiry requires much more than having the wherewithal to devise a question and seek an applicable answer. Rather, it must involve questioning the motives, the rationale, and any potentially obscured biases behind the question. For example: How did I approach the area of inquiry? What factors may have influenced how I framed the question? What biases might I harbor? How do I (or others) know when the question has been fully answered? Through all these levels of inquiry, the individual must remain cognizant of the possibility that new or unforeseen information may arise at any time to cast doubt or to strengthen one's line of thinking. Quite simply, as Candy (1990) and Mezirow (1991) taught us, the critical thinker knows to expect the unexpected and is always ready and willing to reconsider previously held positions. Diane's recommendation was for me to admit my biases and proceed to look at the phenomenon from all angles. She readily illustrated her willingness to do the same with her statements: "Some of your questions brought a different perspective than I normally would have taken myself," and "I started looking at some of the things I was doing that I never would have paid attention to before."

Through my observations, I concluded that each informant understood the essence of critical inquiry and was able to engage in critical thought. Howard demonstrated his grasp of the concept with his observation of filmmaker Michael Moore. He said, "I showed the movie *Bowling for Columbine* as an example of critical-thinking. Here's a guy who goes out and asks those questions that are far outside. He makes up his own questions as he goes and he digs and digs and digs until he finds something." Karl described internal motivations similar to those Howard saw in Michael Moore, in which his desire to see and understand things in a different way accelerated and intensified his use of critical thought. Comparing his experience to those lacking his curiosity, Karl said, "And then you get so far thinking of the world in a diverse, holistic, and idealistic way, that all of a sudden it's hard to even understand people who have gone the other way."

Despite clear examples of being able to understand and appreciate the concept of critical inquiry, I was unable to determine the extent to which their abilities rose to a level of scholarship, loosely defined as the possession of considerable academic knowledge acquired through a rigorous and systematic approach. Even with my benchmarks, the assessment of critical thinking ability can be quite tricky. If I were to learn that each informant was ultimately able to earn his or her respective degree, the critical challenge before me would be to avoid the assumption that having successfully completed a program in which critical inquiry plays a central role automatically qualifies the individual as a scholar in that or any other area of a given curriculum. True, earning a doctorate or master's makes the argument in favor of scholarship compelling. To simply accept a diploma as proof of one's scholarship, however, is to proceed uncritically. Regardless, the commentary on adult education offered by each of the informants was at minimum well informed.

A Few Surprises

Before our interviews, I had never met any of the informants. Nevertheless, the majority of their experiences were not particularly surprising to me. As with the books on AD/HD, I experienced a sense of familiarity with what they were willing to share. What was, perhaps, the biggest surprise did not result from what was said. Rather, it was the unintended result of our integrated communication experiences. Foreshadowing the first incident was Marianne's admission of an ongoing battle regarding the impulse to finish other people's sentences whenever they spoke too slowly for her. My recordings confirmed this, as she made a habit of finishing numerous sentences for me. I too experience some frustration (if not anxiety) with people who speak slowly or haltingly, and with those who regularly repeat themselves. At such times, I often feel trapped. Unlike Marianne, I am generally able to keep from speaking for them. Interestingly, the recording showed that after having had a number of my sentences completed by her, I began completing a few of hers in return. Although I seldom offered more than a few words at a time, I did manage to mangle what might otherwise have been several informative passages. Once transcribed, I approached those exchanges with painstaking caution to avoid confusing any of my own assumptions for hers.

Two of Diane's struggles involved dyslexia and hearing spoken words clearly. A complication was that she would often draw a blank when searching for the right word. In response, Diane periodically resorted to expressing herself with gestures—a predicament I too experience, but with less regularity. Upon first listen to the recordings of our interviews, the frequency of what appeared to be dead air—punctuated by laughter—surprised me. Upon closer inspection, I realized that our dialog was essentially without pause (just as I had remembered it). Astoundingly, we kept shifting between body language and verbally communication. As for the laughter, I simply enjoyed Diane's sense of humor—one of the positive traits Kelly and Ramundo (1993) have associated with AD/HD. That laugher should not be discounted for fear of overlooking something of potential importance was yet another piece of advice offered by Siedman (1998). The reader may recall that in addition to Diane's ability to understand non-English speaking persons was Karl's assertion that he too was a keen observer of the unspoken message. Such empathic ability to sense what others are feeling is an attribute Weiss (1997) insightfully observed within the lives of persons with AD/HD.

Unlike Marianne, who was well aware of her habit of cutting people off, and unlike Diane, who learned to accept that she possessed a unique way of knowing, Howard did not specifically mention his tendency to drift off topic. This did nothing to curtail the behavior, however. Howard's wanderings frequently veered into issues that called for a counselor, more than an interviewer. Then, upon Howard noticing an amorphous ink drawing hanging from my office wall, I absently launched into a rambling account of my days as an art student. That single off-topic exchange lasted nearly eight minutes. The fact that I was as likely to succumb to distractions as Howard provided a shared moment of levity. Although in-depth phenomenological interviewing reserves a place for self-disclosure, there was nothing tactical about my verbal meandering. Howard's digressions, however, continued with regularity and overwhelmingly focused on serious issues within his birth family and his multiple marriages, issues that were inappropriate to our forum. Forewarned of the tendency for some informants to misconstrue the personal nature of the phenomenological interview as counseling, it still took a while before I managed the wherewithal to avert impending digressions. After several redirections aimed at him, Howard exchanged the favor.

Although the breadth of this apparent theme did not become clear until after I began close readings of the transcriptions, because I had over seven months to spend with the recordings before completing the final series of interviews, I was well aware of some of the difficulties I was having as an interviewer. For the final series, I decided to devote more attention to my interviewing style. As previously noted, Karl tended to speak rapidly and with a mixture of enthusiasm and tension. Those who know me well would likely make the same observation of me—at least in certain circumstances. Having made a decision to speak more slowly and with greater deliberation than usual, I avoided the reciprocity that took place between me and the other three.

Another surprise involved the place of religion and spirituality among the informants. Admittedly, these issues did not enter my mind as I developed my research proposal. Both Marianne and Diane attended Catholic schools through high school graduation. For Marianne, a fear of nuns provided her with an early motivation to meet school expectations. Later, the highly structured environment played a significant role in keeping a teenaged Marianne from engaging in reckless behaviors. For Diane, church and spirituality featured prominently during each of her interviews. Depressed and contemplating suicide as a teenager, Diane credited her belief in Hell as the actionable deterrent. Years later, an observation that the learning needs of adults in the Bible study classes she taught were being poorly addressed helped to steer Diane toward adult education. She cited her belief in God as her primary source of determination. Although Howard did not mention having attended a church-affiliated school, he was the son of a Protestant minister whose sermons of The New Testament opened Howard's eyes to the concepts of equality and social justice. Howard also spent several years in pursuit of becoming a minister before talking himself out of it. In contrast to the others, Karl had almost nothing to say about the role of religion or spirituality in his life. Nonetheless, I did learn that he attended parochial school through the end of eighth grade.

Critical Self-Inquiry

It is clear that a couple of assumptions regarding the characteristics of a narrowly defined subset of learners helped to give direction to my research. What may yet be unclear is the extent to which these assumptions were aligned with expectations born of an identifiable set of prior experiences (such as those appearing in my autobiographic learning profile) or to such a wide conglomeration of prior experiences and understandings that the whole might better be described as culturally-derived instincts. Brookfield's (1986) concept of the experiential lens is instructive for someone seeking to understand the great influential power of experience. It is through the experiential lens that all incoming information is absorbed. It is also through this lens that people observe the outside world. As humans, we like to describe and explain; we seek to understand. I accept that my experiential lens is made of everything I have ever experienced as well as every meaning I have ever assigned (regardless of accuracy). I know that every pass through adds thickness and curvature. Whereas having accumulated a vast set of experiences can be quite useful when faced with a novel situation, the larger one's experiential base, the higher the likelihood of potentially influential minutiae slipping past one's cognizance. For this reason (and others previously discussed) it was critical for me to establish boundaries during my quest for knowledge. I have fully documented what there was for me to learn directly from the informants. What remains for me to examine is the impact of my close identification with the subjects of this study. Four questions are essential in order to proceed.

1.   What factors led to my topic of inquiry?

2.   What factors may have influenced how I framed the question?

3.   What factors may have influenced how I sought the information?

4.   What factors may have influenced how I interpreted the new information?

Enrollment in the *Learning How to Learn* course was a breakthrough semester for me in terms of learning how to organize my previous encounters with formal education. That I took the course was important. When I took it, was likely as important. Shortly after the course ended, I received my official diagnosis. Soon after, I experienced the private testing room where I was able to experiment with a myriad of coping mechanisms, learning strategies, and just plain "issues," unrestrained. I described the experience as liberating. It also provided an excellent source of material for reflection. Once I passed the qualifying exam, my department officially identified me as a doctoral candidate. This allowed me the freedom to focus on areas of personal interest, most prominently, who I was as a learner and more specifically, who I was as an adult learner diagnosed with AD/HD.

Despite my fascination with a number of texts about AD/HD in adulthood, I became increasingly disappointed, as the intended audience seemed to be those seeking ways to cope or those striving to sharpen their diagnostic and/or counseling skills. I was initially excited upon finding a website that catered to doctoral students with AD/HD struggling through the dissertation process. Once I discovered that its primary function was to offer suggestions, I was again disappointed. My search was for something else. I came across a number of clinician-authors diagnosed with AD/HD. Although some texts shared personal stories, they generally lacked in-depth self-analysis. By this time, I had concluded that self-knowledge acquired through purposeful acts of reflection on learning was key to sharpening my own ability to self-regulate. Like the informants who found little value in the self-help-styled books they had read, I too sought a different approach: to see where my ideas concerning self-analysis fit within the larger discussion of adults with AD/HD.

During *Learning How to Learn* I began to realize that the context I sought might not exist. If my observations were accurate, then perhaps I would have to find a way to create the comparative context I sought. Describing an alternative degree program for adult learners offered through Chicago's DePaul University, Lynch (1990) described the benefits of educational autobiographies (a component of the *Learning How to Learn* course offered at Northern Illinois University). According to Lynch, the autobiographical process helps the individual to view his or her experiences as legitimate and can serve to help unify new learning with pre-existing knowledge. In apparent agreement, King and Magolda (1996) observed a close relation between the ways in which individuals create knowledge and how they perceive themselves. Although reflective self-examination certainly can lead to greater self-knowledge, the outcome cannot be absolutely assured. Whereas the destination may be self-knowledge, how does a person know whether he possesses true knowledge or merely the perception of possession? In response, I envisioned an approach and decided to experiment with it.

In order to gain a sense of perspective on my efforts to acquire a high level of self-aware knowledge, I would seek others who shared not only my root condition (having AD/HD), but who shared a similar background in education. As it was a graduate degree in adult education that opened the door to self-regulated learning for me, I would need to locate others enrolled in similar programs. To decrease the likelihood of mistaking perception for knowledge, I would also need to explore my assumptions of what it meant to experience a life through the lens of AD/HD. Likewise; I would need the others to do the same. Fortuitously, my plans coincided with having to submit a dissertation idea for my final doctoral course. What began as an effort to better understand myself was to become a research proposal to better understand those with whom I identified. Even though I had not considered phenomenology while drafting my rough proposal, I was quite aware of the danger of implanting previously held assumptions within the findings. Personally convinced that I would find a way, I had to convince others of the same. Still unaware of the in-depth phenomenological interviewing method, my inclination was to include self-observations made before gathering data as a preface. I had also planned to feature my personal understanding of the study within a postscript. Recalling my experience of the private testing room and my disinterest in so-called self-help books, I decided to focus my inquiry on the development of compensatory strategies rather than on the strategies themselves. Having perceived myself as a process-oriented educator helped to strengthen my investment in this approach. Mindful of the avoidance behaviors rightly attributed to adults with AD/HD, I wanted to know more about the relationship between the self-efficacy of these adults and their levels of achievement.

Having placed greater value on the acquisition of knowledge than on securing support for an agenda, I made a conscious effort to avoid implanting unexamined influences on my findings. Once introduced to phenomenology, I trusted that the method would lead me to whatever meanings there were.

Revisiting the Central Question

The central question sought to understand the meanings graduate students of adult education programs diagnosed with AD/HD in adulthood made of their experiences with formal learning and what impact these meanings have had on how each has come to understand him or herself as a learner. While investigating the literature, three strands emerged as most relevant. For each, my plan was to provide information sufficient to give prospective readers the basic conceptual framework necessary to evaluate the value of my conclusions. For the introduction to adult learning, I relied heavily upon the principles of andragogy, and to a lesser degree, Lindeman's (1926) ideas on adult education. For reader convenience, I have summarized the combined assumptions here.

Adults have a psychological need to be self-directing. They seek new information as it becomes necessary, placing deeper meaning on what they learn experientially (as opposed to passively). They assess learning situations in terms of the timeliness and effectiveness of their application. They place the highest degree of importance on intrinsic rewards, of which finding illumination in informed living may be of the greatest value.

The high regard each of the informants expressed for program flexibility alone suggested their value of self-directed learning. Each also saw their degree as a necessity for professional advancement. For Diane and Howard, the degree would open doors; for Karl and Marianne, it would mean increased income at their present jobs. For all of them, the concept of a timely application extended through their anticipated graduation dates. Nevertheless, each provided examples of how their current programs affected their present lives, from experiences that promote heightened self-esteem (Diane and Howard) to epiphanies that allow one to see education from an entirely new perspective (Karl). Despite the awareness that job-security, promotion, and increased pay likely provided the biggest argument for enrollment, the shared sense of personal satisfaction and of being better able to contribute to society-at-large addressed andragogy's fifth assumption. Furthermore, each of the informants described features of their respective programs that were pivotal (if not transformative) in terms of improved self-understanding, heightened levels of self-acceptance, and a broadened perspective regarding the diverse world in which we all live and learn.

The three doctoral students all described having taken a course that taught critical thinking and/or learning how to learn strategies. Shortly after earning my doctoral degree, I learned that Howard, too, completed a course of similar content. From the reconstructed experiences of Marianne, Diane, and Karl, it seemed apparent that their programs offered courses with similar content. Tellingly, Drs. Niemi and Roth observed that the content of graduate programs in adult continuing education tended to influence students to increase their ability to control learning through self-regulation.

The reader may recall my discussion of the apparent emphasis on self-regulation in adult education graduate programs. Yet, there exists the question of whether or not persons diagnosed with AD/HD are able to reliably manage the complexities of self-regulated learning upon command (Marone and Johnston, 2002), especially when the task lacks intrinsic value. Difficulty with tuning out environmental stimuli, blocking intrusive thoughts, having the sense of being overwhelmed, and simply working much more slowly than others are all descriptive of experiences common to the AD/HD mind (Fisher, 1998). Even for individuals with impressive aptitudes for self-awareness, lengthy histories wrought with frustration can lead those diagnosed to place greater value on the avoidance of further frustration, than on finding ways beyond it (Bramer, 1996). With regard to the informants to this study, personal drive proved to be the stronger motivator.

The reader should recall numerous informant examples of invalidating environments (and persons) within formal education settings. Nevertheless, each informant found varying ways to navigate what could, at times, be very unforgiving settings, whether real (the verbal degradation of Diane and Howard) or imagined (Karl's unawareness that teachers actually taught the material during class). Despite the commonality of their motivations—including a shared commitment to the ideals of social justice and equality—and apart from their intrinsic drive of largely unknown origins, the impact of formal education during their youth was diverse. For Marianne, it was about keeping up with her peers. For Diane, it was about proving something to those who doubted her (including herself). Howard's central motivation was rooted in avoidance turned escapism. For Karl, it was an intrapersonal quest to see how far he could push himself. Highly intriguing was the extent to which each found ways to compensate with limited assistance from teachers and parents (Whereas Karl's father did provide the structure for his learning, it was Karl who quickly took personal ownership.).

I also found that the collective drive to actualize one's potential led to a great variety of coping mechanisms and learning strategies. Again, despite similarities in devising their own methods of compensation, each went about it in his or her way. Howard's need to escape continued to be an influence on what symptoms he chose to combat and how. When determined to face his issues (such as passing his Navy exam), Howard relied on such uninventive techniques as keeping the textbook handy. When escapism was the motivation, Howard showed some creativity (such as, deflecting criticism with humor).

Early on, Karl discovered that he could teach himself. Thereafter, he relied on what appeared to be a rigid and very effective system for learning. Even after many years of using his system, once the curriculum and the student-to-instruc-tor/student-to-student relationship changed (as it did when he began taking courses in adult education), Karl was able to reinvent his way of looking at the social sciences, having undergone a transformation that allowed him to see its lack of rigidity from a new perspective. Program flexibility was not a sign of infe-riority, as he had initially thought. Rather, it was a foundation for opportunity. Whereas Karl's compensatory learning strategies took a conscious and sweeping approach, Diane's took a conscious, piecemeal approach, with all sorts of self-styled coping mechanisms and learning strategies, each in response to some fairly specific aspect of her need for compensation. Although Marianne offered a few examples of being deliberately proactive, the bulk of her compensatory strategies seemed almost to have sprung ready-made from her subconscious mind. By tak-ing her laptop computer and spreading her materials all over her bed, Marianne has been able to avoid the sense of discomfort otherwise experienced in situations where remaining seated for long periods was the expectation. Unlike Diane, Mar-ianne's use of a conventional workspace would contribute to her tendency to lose track of necessary supplies. In this way Marianne's expression of, or response to, one symptom (criterion [g] for inattention) inadvertently addressed a second symptom (criterion [b] for hyperactivity) in a helpful way.

With respect to varying degrees of self-awareness, heightened self-awareness without compensation tended to lower self-esteem. Heightened self-awareness with effective compensation tended to increase self-efficacy. Lidner and Harris (1992) suggested that whether or not the self-aware learner is consistently able to achieve success, he does nevertheless maintain a sense of ownership in the process and outcome and is likely able to see beyond the present failure towards the next possible success. That Marianne was able to describe her inability to narrow her research topic in a generally upbeat way lends support to this perspective. The reader may also recall Marianne's optimistic assessment that medications would hold little value for her given all that she has been able to figure out without them.

What is readily apparent is that the three doctoral students achieved a high level of accurate and reliable self-knowledge. Whereas the master's student also achieved a respectable level of reliability, it was unclear how accurate his initial self-assessments were. Certainly, he was far less forgiving of his perceived failings than the other three. Marianne, Diane, and Karl all mentioned either a critical thinking course or a course that focused on learning how to learn that was pivotal with regard to their increased levels of self-understanding and self-acceptance.

Perhaps Howard's dampened ability to accurately assess himself was the result of having been abused as a child, or in response to his long history of having critiqued his own life through the experiential lens of perceived failure.

As discussed, the ability to develop compensatory strategies hinged on more than accurate self-assessment. Karl, for example, was keenly aware of how he learned best in formal settings. Yet, the one-size-fits-most strategy that worked so well in academic settings left him floundering in a motel room full of fishing supplies. Nearly every time Diane discovered some idiosyncrasy with regard to her way of knowing, she found some way to cope. Howard learned to identify those elements of formal learning where he had the most to offer. Although Karl and Diane discovered the benefits of caffeine, only Howard chose the use of medication as a strategy. In short, each of the informants managed to employ strategies that increased their effectiveness as learners and increased their overall self-efficacy. In having done so, each has had successful experiences with self-regulated learning (albeit, with one catch). With the exception of Howard, who occasionally ingested an extra dose of medication when needed, the other three lacked a similarly dependable way to boost self-regulation upon command.

What I must not leave out of this discussion is the potential impact of believing in the possibility of change. Texts, such as those authored by Thom Hartmann, offer encouraging alternate perspectives. In place of symptoms, Hartmann (1997) conceptualized AD/HD characteristics merely as traits. The value I place on Hartmann's conceptualization of the hunter is linked to the process of reframing past experience. Following diagnosis, those with AD/HD have an opportunity to revisit a lifetime's worth of frustration. They have a way to make sense of their history of unseen impediments, their failure to live up to their raw potential, or their need to expend so much more energy than others to achieve a comparable level of success. My own experience with diagnosis was one of near-jubilation. Bristling within the pages of nearly every book that I found written on the subject of AD/HD in adulthood were dead-on descriptions of what I had experienced many times over, stories brimming with rapid-fire futility mixed with episodic hilarity. Long after the thrill of discovery and after learning how to better manage my symptoms, I took time to consider some of the previously unrealized ramifications of having a diagnosable disorder. Because it affects cognitive functioning, AD/HD cannot help but to leave its imprint on the whole person. Furthermore, if the condition itself is inherently undesirable, maintaining a positive outlook can be tricky. Whether or not the conception of a hunter in a world filled with farmers ever achieves critical acceptance from the psychiatric community may be much less important overall than the sense of personal comfort Hartmann's ideas provide. In terms of what this has to do with learning, I remind the reader that once an individual has come to define himself as lacking ability, or has developed low self-efficacy, he is likely to bring this defeatist mindset to new learning situations. The ability to reexamine past experience in light of new information can help the person with AD/HD work to dispel some of the negative self-perceptions that may compound and complicate actual symptoms. Once an individual becomes aware of his own limitations, he is better suited to compensate for them. Such transcendence is a vital prerequisite to effective learning.

Organizing the Essential Meanings

What this study has to offer academe is a set of interpretively rich data drawn from the collective experiences of four insightful informants. Throughout, I sought to learn how those at the heart of this study understood their experiences related to coping, strategizing, learning, and the acquiring of self-knowledge. As I neared the end of the dissertation process and with graduation in sight, I became aware of the potential for these meanings to serve as foundational assumptions towards a model of graduate students diagnosed with AD/HD. My strategy is simple. It is merely to organize a synthesis of the meanings into a coherent and accessible form, summarized in Table 1.

The first column, "Learner Characteristics," identifies character traits possessed by each of the informants (to varying degrees) from their earliest experiences with formal learning, through the present. Each shared examples that served to illuminate their curiosity and their intrinsic sense of motivation. Likewise, each was able to describe how their symptoms (or AD/HD-like behaviors) affected their academic performance as well as their overall scholastic experience. Although the ability to use one symptomatic behavior to combat another was not nearly so visible during their combined recollections of youth, because the phenomenon frequently occurred without overt awareness, the ability is best described as a characteristic intrinsic to the individual.

The second column, "Pedagogical Experience," identifies the primary point of experiential divergence within the pedagogical environment. Those whose AD/HD (and/or AD/HD-like) behaviors failed to draw attention were not saddled with the unproductive invalidations received by those whose behaviors were more visible, and therefore deemed to be in conflict with the pedagogical model of formal education.

Table 1.

Graduate Students of Adult Education Programs Diagnosed with Attention-Deficit/Hyperactivity Disorder in Adulthood

Learner Characteristics	Pedagogical Experience	Pedagogical Outcomes	Adult Education	Adult Education Outcomes
Innate sense of curiosity Persistent intrinsic motivation to learn Symptomatic expression of AD/HD Self-reliant ability to cope with and compensate for problematic symptoms of AD/HD	Values institution's wants, needs, and preferred modes of instruction Validates adherence to institution's standards Invalidates visible symptomatic expression of AD/HD (esp. those symptoms which violate standards)	Outcome A Lack of external invalidation allows for development of non-avoidance-based problem-solving, which heightens self-efficacy Emergence of AD/HD symptoms used for coping and/or compensation (with/without cognizance of) is valued by learner according to whether or not his/her goals are met Outcome B Presence of external invalidation prompts development of avoidance-based problem-solving and internal polarization (self-validation versus self-invalidation) Emergence of AD/HD symptoms used for coping and/or compensation (with/without cognizance of) is valued by learner according to whether (external or self-) invalidation increases or decreases	Values learner's wants, needs, and preferred styles of learning Promotes self-regulated learning Promotes critical thinking Validates adult's growth as a learner	Outcome A & B Gains greater awareness of one's own intrinsic motivation Strengthens critical thinking and self-regulated learning, which heightens self-efficacy Increases use of (and experimentation with) AD/HD symptoms for coping, compensating, strategizing, and learning Outcome A With emphasis on problem-solving and self-acceptance (as a learner) goals more steadily realized Outcome B Given ongoing struggles with internal polarization (self-acceptance versus shame) goals less steadily realized (with growth haphazardly punctuated by setbacks)

The third column, "Pedagogical Outcomes," highlights the divergent out-comes for those who escaped invalidation from those who did not. Those in the first group (Outcome A) managed as best they could, largely unaware of the extent to which their academic experiences fell outside the norm. Successes rein-forced belief in their own abilities, thus heightening self-efficacy. Unable to avoid invalidation, those in the second group (Outcome B) learned to invalidate them-selves. As a result, much of their energy was spent attempting to avoid further external invalidation. For them, success served to strengthen their resolve to ensure that their "differences" remained hidden.

The fourth column, "Adult Education," identifies those aspects of formal graduate programs in adult education mentioned by the informants as being the most helpful with regard to increasing their self-understanding, their effectiveness as learners, and their wherewithal to accept themselves as they are.

The fifth and final column, "Adult Education Outcomes," serves two func-tions. The first is to highlight the areas of personal growth experienced by all four of the informants, each of whom gave some of the credit to their respective adult education programs. The second is to highlight the power and the longevity of invalidation's stranglehold upon those with unconventional ways of learning and knowing, as administered by the very people entrusted with the responsibility to educate young learners.

11

EXITING THE MAZE

In the first chapter, I shared my interest in meeting each of Creswell's (1997) three standards for qualitative research. From conception through publication, this project has lasted nearly six years, during which time I have witnessed a literary expansion regarding college students living with AD/HD. Even so, comparatively little has touched upon graduate students in general or doctoral candidates in particular. With each successive layer of exactitude, I pushed my research ever further from the mainstream. It is therefore apparent that I have met at least two of Creswell's standards. I have addressed an issue with an understudied group, and I have begun to fill an existing void within the literature. With respect to my remaining aspiration—the establishment of a new line of thinking—I am undecided. Replace the word "thinking" with the word "questioning," however, and the possibility almost certainly rises.

I would hope that the essential meanings encapsulated at the end of Chapter 9, fleshed out in Chapter 10, and organized in Table 1 suggest one or more possibilities for further research. Perhaps someone will focus on the idea of putting phenomenological bracketing to work as a means to improving self-knowledge. Maybe conceptualizing symptoms as behaviors that—through self-regulation—can be fashioned into effective learning strategies will generate new lines of questioning. Then again, I would be just as pleased to have a teacher simply think twice about sending an adventurous child back to his or her assigned seat, cognizant that being "on the go" does not necessarily imply that learning is not taking place. Whatever happens next, if this new line of thinking or questioning is to have meaning—or better yet, power—then it the reader who must think, question, and act.

My purpose in conducting this study was to search for meaning. Whether or not the journey proves useful to others, it has been of the highest value to me. I took great interest in listening to the informants reconstruct their learning experiences and wrangle embedded meanings from within. I also savored the experience of illuminating aspects of my own sense of being, many of which were somewhat obscured, even to me. Although this chapter of my life is closing, my own quest for self-knowledge remains very much an active pursuit. I relish the challenge of keeping abreast of who I am—knowing that self-awareness takes ongoing and critical self-observation. Marianne, Diane, Howard, and Karl have shown this to be true.

Recall a sixth-grade boy, who learned to despise himself for his failures in school, and who grew up to help disadvantaged youth struggling towards college. Recall another young man suddenly realizing that teachers actually taught things during the day, yet having such an accomplished system for self-directed learning that he knew he could afford to ignore them anyway. Recall two teenaged girls in Catholic high school, both having devised a wide assortment of coping skills and learning strategies to work through their myriad of difficulties. One went largely unnoticed by the teachers and in a way unnoticed to herself. The other, who could not skip, who could not distinguish left from right, and who could not help but to be noticed and judged harshly by others, managed to fight off her own harsh self-assessments. Whether they possessed an array of methods to remain afloat, one all-encompassing learning strategy, or a few sporadic insights and bursts of self-respect, they shared one very important experience of the self-as-learner, they all held a vision of themselves as able and have pursued this common vision with true dignity.

APPENDIX

DIAGNOSTIC CRITERIA FOR ATTENTION-DEFICIT/ HYPERACTIVITY DISORDER

Diagnostic criteria for
Attention-Deficit/Hyperactivity Disorder

A. Either (1) or (2):

(1) six (or more) of the following symptoms of inattention have persisted for at least 6 months to a degree that is maladaptive and inconsistent with developmental level:

Inattention

(a) often fails to give close attention to details or makes careless mistakes in schoolwork, work, or other activities

(b) often has difficulty sustaining attention in tasks or play activities

(c) often does not seem to listen when spoken to directly

(d) often does not follow through on instructions and fails to finish schoolwork, chores, or duties in the workplace (not due to oppositional behavior or failure to understand instructions)

(e) often has difficulty organizing tasks and activities

(f) often avoids, or dislikes, or is reluctant to engage in tasks that require sustained mental effort (such as schoolwork or homework)

(g) often loses things necessary for tasks or activities (e.g., toys, school assignments, pencils, books, or tools)

(h) is often easily distracted by extraneous stimuli

(i) is often forgetful in daily activities

(2) six (or more) of the following symptoms of hyperactivity-impulsivity have persisted for at least 6 months to a degree that is maladaptive and inconsistent with developmental level:

Hyperactivity

(a) often fidgets with hands or feet or squirms in seat

(b) often leaves seat in classroom or other situations in which remaining seated is expected

(c) often runs about or climbs excessively in situations in which it is inappropriate (in adolescents or adults, may be limited to subjective feelings of restlessness)

(d) often has difficulty playing or engaging in leisure activities quietly

(e) is often "on the go" or acts as if "driven by a motor"

(f) often talks excessively

Impulsivity

(g) often blurts out answers before questions have been completed

(h) often has difficulty awaiting turn

(i) often interrupts or intrudes on others (e.g., butts into conversations or games)

B. Some hyperactive-impulsive or inattentive symptoms that caused impairment were present before age 7 years.

C. Some impairment from the symptoms is present in two or more settings (e.g., at school [or work] and at home).

D. There must be clear evidence of clinically significant impairment in social, academic, or occupational functioning.

E. The symptoms do not occur exclusively during the course of a Pervasive Developmental Disorder, Schizophrenia, or other Psychotic Disorder and are not better accounted for by another mental disorder (e.g., Mood Disorder, Anxiety

Disorder, Dissociative Disorder, or a Personality Disorder) (DSM-IV-TR, 2000, pp. 92-93).

REFERENCES

Alvesson, M., & Skoldberg, K. (2000). *Reflexive methodology*. London: Sage.

Amen, D. G. (2001). *Healing ADD: The breakthrough program that allows you to see and heal the 6 types of ADD*. New York: G. P. Putnam's Sons.

American Psychiatric Association. (1980). *Diagnostic and statistical manual of mental disorders* (3rd ed.). Washington, DC: Author.

American Psychiatric Association. (1987). *Diagnostic and statistical manual of mental disorders* (3rd ed., rev.). Washington, DC: Author.

American Psychiatric Association. (2000). *Diagnostic and statistical manual of mental disorders* (4th ed. Text Revision). Washington, DC: Author.

Armstrong, T. (1994). *Multiple intelligences in the classroom*. Alexandria: Association for Supervision and Curriculum Development.

Author. (1989). *The oxford English dictionary* (2nd ed., Vols. 3-18). In J. A. H. Murray, H. Bradley, W. A. Craigi, C. T. Onions, & R. W. Burchfield (Eds.), Oxford: Clarendon Press.

Bandura, A. (1993). Perceived self-efficacy in cognitive development and functioning. *Educational Psychologist*, 28, 117-148.

Bandura, A. (1995). Exercise of personal and collective efficacy in changing societies. In Bandura (Ed.), *Self-efficacy in changing societies* (pp. 1-45). Cambridge: Cambridge University Press.

Bandura, A. (1997) Self-efficacy: *The exercise of control*. New York: W. H. Freedman and Company.

Barkley, R. A. (1997). *ADHD and the nature of self-control*. New York: The Guilford Press.

Biggs, S. H. (1995). Neuropsychological and psychoeducational testing in the evaluation of the ADD adult. In K. G. Nadeau (Ed.), *A comprehensive guide to attention deficit disorder in adults: Research, diagnosis, treatment* (pp. 109-131). New York: Brunner/Mazel Publishers.

Bramer, J. S. (1996). *Succeeding in college with attention deficit disorders: Issues and strategies for students, counselors, and educators.* Plantation: Specialty Press Inc.

Brown, T. (1995). Differential diagnosis of ADD versus ADHD in adults. In K.G. Nadeau (Ed.), *A comprehensive guide to attention deficit disorder in adults: Research, diagnosis, treatment* (pp. 93-108). New York: Brunner/Mazel Publishers.

Brown, T. B. (2000), Emerging understandings of attention-deficit disorders and comorbidities. In T. B. Brown (Ed.), *Attention-deficit disorders and comorbidities in children, adolescents, and adults* (pp. 93-108). Arlington: American Psychiatric Press, Inc.

Brookfield, S. (1986). *Understanding and facilitating adult learning.* San Francisco: Jossey-Bass.

Brookfield, S. (1990). Expanding knowledge about how we learn. In R. M. Smith (Ed.), *Learning to learn across the lifespan* (pp. 327-345). San Francisco: Jossey-Bass.

Brooks, R. B., & Goldstein, S. (2006). Fostering resilience. In P. Hollingsworth (Ed.), *The new CHADD information and resource guide to AD/HD: 2006-2007 edition* (pp. 137-141). New York: Harper Collins.

Candy, P. C. (1990). How people learn to learn. In R. M. Smith (Ed.), *Learning to learn across the lifespan* (pp. 30-63). San Francisco: Jossey-Bass.

Cooper, M. K., Gibson, S., Hanes, L., & Sundre, S. K. (2000). *An invitation to conversation: The process and promise of phenomenology.* Paper presented at the Midwest Research-to Practice Conference in Adult, Community, and Continuing Education, University of Wisconsin, Madison, WI.

Creswell, J. W. (1997). *Qualitative inquiry and research design: Choosing among the five traditions.* Thousand Oaks: SAGE Publications, Inc.

Dewey, J. (1916). *Democracy and education.* New York: Macmillan.

Diane [pseudo.]. (2004). [Auditory response to interview series]. Unpublished raw data.

Evans, J., & Miller, M. T. (1990). Adult learner characteristics among graduate Education students: Comparison by academic discipline. In McMillan, F. C. (2003). *A qualitative study of adult women in a northeast Tennessee community college* (Doctoral dissertation, East Tennessee University, 2003).

Fisher, B. C. (1998). *Attention deficit disorder misdiagnosis: Approaching ADD from a brain-behavior/neuropsychological perspective for assessment and treatment.* Boca Raton: CRC Press.

Freire, P. (1972) *Pedagogy of the Oppressed.* Harmondsworth: Penguin.

Furjanic, S. W., & Trotman, L. A. (2000). *Turning training into learning.* New York: American Management Association.

Gibbons, M. (1990). A working model of the learning-how-to-learn process. In R. M. Smith (Ed.), *Learning to learn across the lifespan* (pp. 64-97). San Francisco: Jossey-Bass.

Goldman, L. S., Genel, M., Bezman, R. J., & Slanetz, P. J. (1998). *Diagnosis and treatment of attention-deficit/hyperactivity disorder in children and adolescents.* Council on Scientific Affairs, American Medical Association. JAMA, 279, 1100-7.

Goodman, R., & Stevenson, J. (1989). A twin study of hyperactivity II: The aetiological role of genes, family relationships, and prenatal adversity. *Journal of Child Psychology and Psychiatry*, 30, 691-709.

Hallowell, E. (1995). Psychotherapy of adult attention deficit disorder. In K. G. Nadeau (Ed.), *A comprehensive guide to attention deficit disorder in adults: Research, diagnosis, treatment* (pp. 146-167). New York: Brunner/Mazel Publishers.

Hart, M. (1992). *Working and educating for life: Feminist and international perspectives on adult education.* London: Routledge.

Hartmann, T. (1997). *Attention deficit disorder: A different perspective.* Grass Valley: Underwood Books.

Hoban, S., & Hoban, G. (2004). Self-esteem, self-efficacy and self-directed learning. *International Journal of Self-Directed Learning*, 1(2), 7-25.

Howard [pseudo.]. (2004). [Auditory response to interview series]. Unpublished raw data.

Ilsley, P., & Krasemann, K. (2003). *Phenomenological methodology* [On-Line]. Retrieved: 7/12/2006. Available: http://www.uta.fi/laitokset/aktk/jatko/Phenomenology.doc.

Jehng, J. J., Johnson, S. D., & Anderson, R. C. (1993). Schooling and students' epistemological beliefs about learning. *Contemporary Educational Psychology*, 18, 23-35.

Jones, G. C., Kalivoda, K. S., & Higbee, J. L., (1997). College students with attention deficit disorder. *NASPA Journal*, 34(4), 262-274.

Karl [pseudo.]. (2005). [Auditory response to interview series]. Unpublished raw data.

Katz, L. J. (2006). College success; Accommodations and strategies that work. In P. Hollingsworth (Ed.). *The new CHADD information and resource guide to AD/HD*; 2006-2007 Edition (pp. 93-97). New York: Harper Collins.

Kelly, K., & Ramundo, P. (1993). *You mean I'm not lazy, stupid, or crazy?! A self-help book for adults with attention deficit disorder.* Cincinnati: Tyrell and Jerem Press.

King, P. M., & Magolda, M. B. (1996). A developmental perspective on learning. *Journal of College Student Development*, 37(2), 163-173.

Knapp, C. E. (1996). *Just beyond the classroom.* Charleston: Clearinghouse on Rural Education and Small Schools.

Knowles, M. (1980). *The modern practice of adult education: From pedagogy to andragogy* (2nd ed.). New York: Cambridge Books.

Kremer-Haylon, L., & Tillema, H. H. (1999). Self-regulated learning in the context of teacher education. *Teaching and Teacher Education*, 15, 507-522.

Lahey, B. B. (1998). *ADHD as a disorder in children, adolescents, and adults: Current diagnostic schema/core dimensions.* A paper presented at National Institutes of Health Consensus Development Conference on Diagnosis and Treatment of Attention Deficit Hyperactivity Disorder at Bethesda, MD.

Latham, P. S., & Latham, P. H. (1995). Legal rights of the ADD adult. In K. G. Nadeau (Ed.), *A comprehensive guide to attention deficit disorder in adults: Research, diagnosis, treatment* (pp. 337-351). New York: Brunner/Mazel Publishers.

Latham, P. S., & Latham, P. H. (1997). *Attention deficit disorder and the law* (2nd ed.). Washington DC: JKL Communications.

Lidner, R., & Harris, B. (1992). *Self-regulated learning and academic achievement in college students.* Paper presented at the American Educational Research Association Annual Meeting, San Francisco, CA.

Lindeman, E. C. (1926). *The Meaning of Adult Education.* New York: New Republic.

Linehan, M. M. (1993). *Cognitive-behavioral treatment of borderline personality disorder.* New York: The Guilford Press.

Linksman, R. (1996). *How to learn anything quickly.* Seacaucus: Carol Publishing Group.

Lynch, A. Q. (1990). Helping college students take charge of their education. In R. M. Smith (Ed.), *Learning to learn across the lifespan* (pp. 219-246). San Francisco: Jossey-Bass.

Magolda, M. B. (2002). Epistemological reflection: The evolution of Epistemological assumptions from age 18 to 30. In B. K. Hofer, & P. R. Pintrich (Eds.), *Personal epistemology: The psychology of beliefs about knowledge and knowing* (pp. 89-118). Mahwah: Erlbaum.

Mapou, R. L. (2001, Summer/Fall). *Research on learning disabilities and attention-deficit/hyperactivity disorder in adults.* Division 40 Newsletter.

Marianne [pseudo.]. (2004). [Auditory response to interview series]. Unpublished raw data.

Marone, D., & Johnston, E. (2002). *Teaching students who have a learning disability: Strategies for faculty, tutors, and learning instructors* [On-Line]. Weingarten Learning Resource Center, University of Pennsylvania. Retrieved: 2/14/06. Available: http://www.vpul.upenn.edu/lrc/sds.

Maxfield, D. G. (1989). Learning with the whole mind. In R. M. Smith (Ed.), *Learning to learn across the lifespan* (pp. 98-122). San Francisco: Jossey-Bass.

Merriam, S. B., & Caffarella, R. S. (1991) *Learning in adulthood.* San Francisco: Jossey-Bass.

Mezirow, J. (1991). *Transformative dimensions of adult learning.* San Francisco: Jossey-Bass Inc. Publishers.

McMillan, F. C. (2003). *A qualitative study of adult women in a northeast Tennessee community college* (Doctoral dissertation, East Tennessee University, 2003).

Murphy, K. R. (1995). Empowering the adult with ADD. In K. G. Nadeau (Ed.), *A comprehensive guide to attention deficit disorder in adults: Research, diagnosis, treatment* (pp. 135-145). New York: Brunner/Mazel Publishers.

Nadeau, K. G. (1995). *A comprehensive guide to attention deficit disorder in adults: Research, diagnosis, treatment.* New York: Brunner/Mazel Publishers.

Niemi, H. (2002). Active learning: A cultural change needed in teacher education and schools. *Teaching and Teacher Education*, 18, 763-780.

Nigg, J. T., John, O. P., Blaskey, L. G., & Huang-Pollock, C. L., Willcutt, S. P., Hinshaw, S. P., & Pennington, B. (2002). Big five dimensions and ADHD symptoms: Links between personality traits and clinical symptoms. *Journal of Personality and Social Psychology*, 83(2), 451-469.

Parente, R., & Anderson-Parente, J. (1991). *Retraining memory—Techniques and applications.* Houston: CSY Publishing.

Pintrich, P. R. (2000). The role of motivation in self-regulated learning. In P. R. Pintrich, & P. Ruohotie (Eds.), *Conative constructs and self-regulated learning* (pp. 51-66). Hameenlinna: Research Center for Vocational Education.

Polson, C. J. (1993). *Teaching adult students.* IDEA Paper, 29, 1-7.

Quinn, P. O. (2001). *ADD and the college student: A guide for high school and college students with attention deficit disorder.* New York: Magination Press.

Ratey, J. (2001). *A user's guide to the brain: Perception, attention, and the four theaters of the brain.* New York: Vintage Books.

Richard, M. M. (1995a, Spring/Fall). Pathways to success for the college student with ADD: Accommodations and preferred practices. *Journal on Postsecondary Education and Disability*, vol. 11(2-3), 16-30.

Richard, M. M. (1995b). Students with ADD in postsecondary education: Issues in identification and accommodation. In K. G. Nadeau (Ed.), *A comprehensive guide to Attention Deficit Disorder in adults* (pp. 284-307). New York: Brunner-Mazel Publishers.

Richard, M. M., & Chandler, D. (1994). *Student handbook: Student disability services.* Iowa City: The University of Iowa. Student Disability Services.

Sandler, A. D. (1995). Attention deficits and neurodevelopmental variation in older adolescents and adults. In K. G. Nadeau (Ed.), *A comprehensive guide to attention deficit disorder in adults: Research, diagnosis, treatment* (pp. 58-73). New York: Brunner-Mazel Publishers.

Schommer, M. (1998). The influence of age and schooling on epistemological beliefs. *British Journal of Educational Psychology*, 68, 551-562.

Schultz, R. A. (2002). Illuminating realities: A phenomenological view from two underachieving gifted learners. *Roeper Review*, 24(4): 203-212.

Seidman, I. (1998). *Interviewing as qualitative research: A guide for researchers in education and the social services* (2nd ed.). New York: Teachers College Press.

Smith, R. M. (1982). *Learning how to learn.* Cambridge: The Adult Education Company.

Smith, T. E., Roland, C. C., Havens, M. D., & Hoyt, J. A. (1992). *The theory and practice of challenge education*. Dubuque: Kendall/Hunt Publishing Company.

Spiegelberg, H. (1965). *The phenomenological movement*. The Hague: Martinus Nijhoff.

Stanage, S. M. (1987). *Adult education and phenomenological research*. Malabar: Robert E. Krieger Publishing Company.

Swanson, H. L. (1990). Instruction derived from the strategy deficit model: Overview of principles and procedures. In T. Scruggs, & B. Y. L. Wong (Eds.), *Intervention research in learning disabilities* (pp. 34-65). New York: Springer-Verlag.

Thomasson, A. L. (2005). First-person knowledge in phenomenology. In D. W. Smith (Ed.), *Phenomenology and philosophy of the mind* (pp. 115-139). Oxford: Oxford University Press.

Turnbull, S. (2002). Bricolage as an alternative approach to human resource development theory building. *Human Resource Development Review*, 1(1), 111-128.

Wasserstein, J., Wasserstein, A., & Wolf, L. (2001). *Adults with attention deficit hyperactivity disorder (ADHD)*. Arlington, VA: ERIC. Clearinghouse on Disabilities and Gifted Education.

Weiss, L. (1996). *A.D.D. on the job*. Dallas: Taylor Publishing.

Weiss, L. (1997). *Attention deficit disorder in adults: Practical help and understanding* (3rd ed.). Dallas: Taylor Publishing Company.

Willis, C., Hoben, S., & Myette, P. (1995). Devising a supportive climate based on clinical vignettes of college students with Attention Deficit Disorder. *Journal on Postsecondary Education and Disability*, 11(2 & 3).

Winne, P. H. (1995). *Inherent details in self-regulated learning*. Educational Psychologist, 30(4): 173-87.

Wolf, L. (2001). College students with ADHD and other hidden disabilities: Outcomes and interventions. *Annals of the New York Academy of Sciences,* 931, 385-395.

978-0-595-44617-9
0-595-44617-5

www.ingramcontent.com/pod-product-compliance
Lightning Source LLC
Chambersburg PA
CBHW020439290526
45785CB00002B/922